Ukraine 22

Ukraine 22

Ukrainian Writers Respond to War

EDITED BY MARK ANDRYCZYK

PENGUIN BOOKS

PENGUIN BOOKS

UK | USA | Canada | Ireland | Australia
India | New Zealand | South Africa

Penguin Books is part of the Penguin Random House group of companies
whose addresses can be found at global.penguinrandomhouse.com

First published 2023
001

Set in 11/13pt Dante MT Std
Typeset by Jouve (UK), Milton Keynes
Printed and bound in Great Britain by Clays Ltd, Elcograf S.p.A.

The authorized representative in the EEA is Penguin Random House Ireland,
Morrison Chambers, 32 Nassau Street, Dublin D02 YH68

A CIP catalogue record for this book is available from the British Library

ISBN: 978-1-802-06291-5

www.greenpenguin.co.uk

Contents

Contents

Preface

Much of the world has been in awe of Ukrainian women and men over the past year, searching for the source of their bravery and resolve under devastating conditions. How do they continue to fight against all odds while enduring wave after wave of attacks, cruelty and wanton destruction? Much of the drive behind that resolve can be found in these essays, which show that Ukraine's citizens, who are being targeted for annihilation because of their identity, see themselves standing face to face with evil. For them, their battle is a moral and existential choice.

Ukraine 22: Ukrainian Writers Respond to War contains twenty-eight essays written by nine prominent Ukrainian writers and cultural figures, representing different generations and hailing from various regions of Ukraine. The essays were written in the first year after the full-scale Russian invasion of Ukraine on 24 February 2022, and they describe the experience of living amidst war and genocide. Like other accounts of war in other parts of the world during the twentieth century and earlier, they offer stark narratives and capture particular moments during a precarious time. They paint a picture of the events, emotions and philosophical meditations of a people fighting for their right to exist. To best convey this complex milieu, the book offers multiple essays by each author, ordered chronologically instead of by author. Certain threads appear in the essays of several different authors, allowing for multiple approaches to vital issues and giving a layered, expressive view of how life has unfolded during wartime.

The authors explore various themes: they appeal to Europe to better understand the nature of this war – how it does not concern just a single tyrant like Putin but is also about the Russian imperial identity that, unlike other imperial identities over the course of world history, has never undergone decolonization. These writers are appalled both by the atrocities committed by Russian soldiers today and by what they see as a general lack of shock and disgust among the Russian people themselves regarding these crimes. They identify symptoms of this malaise in Russian culture itself and examine how that culture has served to enable, justify and whitewash such behaviour. The authors revisit Ukraine's history and discuss previous struggles for Ukrainian independence, revealing an enduring battle against imperial subjugation that has only now truly become evident to the world. They write about how their lives and the lives of others have been disrupted or even destroyed by the war and how this common struggle has brought Ukrainians from various regions and walks of life closer together. They often look to nature and to literature for guidance, while at the same time realizing that those aesthetic and emotional sources of reassurance and stability have also been greatly affected by the war.

In today's war, Ukrainian artists see it as their duty to use their skills to battle on the cultural front. Reflecting the war in which their authors are living, these essays are sometimes quite raw, and might be unsettling for readers who may not have expected such a forthright depiction of the feelings arising during war. The essays contain horror, rage and confusion, but also empathy and solidarity. These writers are stunned that in this latest attack on Ukraine the Russians themselves regularly announce their genocidal goals and then record their war crimes for the world to see. But in a way they are also encouraged by the fact that Russia's centuries-long attempt to erase the Ukrainian identity has finally caught the world's gaze. It is telling that some of the sharpest reactions to Russians and to their culture come from previously Russophone Ukrainian writers who are well-versed in Russian culture and history. It seems likely that some views expressed in these essays will change over time – some may harden while others may soften. As the war continues, new issues will undoubtedly come to the fore to accompany the foundational ones explored here from the first year of the war.

For the past year, several international writers and artists have been documenting the harshness of the Russian–Ukrainian war in articles and films. They tell stories of people clinging to their humanity despite recurring atrocities. Leading Ukrainian cultural figures, too, have been interpreting the extraordinary circumstances in which they and their fellow citizens have been living through their exceptional artistic talents. *Ukraine 22: Ukrainian Writers Respond to War* gives a global audience the opportunity to read these candid, nuanced essays exploring the existential concerns of Ukrainians under war.

Mark Andryczyk
14 March 2023

War Begins Privately

Taras Prokhasko

24 February 2022

Soon our impressions of war's arrival will transform into personal stories, told with an individual spin by every person who is able to remember them. From this moment – the morning of 24 February – on, everyone will think that they are doing the right thing. People only do that which they can't *not* do. It's tempting to do what others are doing, but the desire to do things your own way is even stronger.

Very soon you will discover that you, nevertheless, did do something wrong. For example, you didn't move the bed where you and your child sleep away from the window, even though you know that it's not just explosions but shattering glass, too, that can scare a child the most. That's the first lesson. Perhaps it would be wise to move it tomorrow. But: firstly, how do you do that without frightening your child? Secondly, whatever happened this morning might not happen again. War is war, but progress ensures that it will always be different from the last time. But here, it's reassuring that everything remains the same, that there is no bread for sale but there is mobile reception. This is very important: such a huge part of us has been transferred into our phones that if they don't work we feel we have lost a part of ourselves. But there is another side to this problem. An uninterrupted phone and internet connection can be exploited in modern war and terrible things can be done with them to confuse and incapacitate us. (In any case, best practice before an apocalypse is to establish alternative ways to contact people you need to be with, whether they are near or far, you will need to be together somehow.)

In general, you need to realize that this war (it could uncynically be called a *voinushka**) is led by a plot. They create literature, a storyline—their own *bylina, skaz, piesn, lietopis, vsieobshchaia istroiia*, great encyclopedia.† No matter how it looks to those watching from the sidelines. They write whatever they want, because 'they'll just keep touting their glory.'

A sketch of that storyline is this: everything is very straightforward. Two proud, distressed, independent countries, whose sovereignties were established by nationwide referendums, have been suffering for eight years now under the hand of a regime that is brutalizing the people's will to freedom with all its might. Finally, the independents, disillusioned by the double standards of the so-called global community, turned to the only power that guarantees truth on earth for help. Of course, the good rush to save the good. This is the way it was done, even by those evil powers that deceptively referred to themselves as good. They were allowed to do so according to that rotting codex, and now all the more so. On top of that, one of the best and most aggressive armies in all of Europe, the Ukrainian army, somehow ended up in the territory of these

---

* A *voinushka* is the word that Russian children use to refer to games that they play.

† A *bylina* is an Old Russian epic poem. *Skaz* is a Russian oral form of narrative. In Old Russian, *piesn* is a song. A *lietopis* is an East Slavic chronicle. *Vsieobshchaia istroiia* is the Russian term for the history of humankind.

independent countries that have been recognized by the world, and has brought death. And so on . . .

Knowing Russian literature, you can imagine subsequent paragraphs about helping hands with no strings attached, about the fact that the enemy must be destroyed. And the righteous world order, when the aggressor's army will not only be neutralized in those deceptively occupied territories, but the lair of its leadership will be infiltrated too.

Their story of the war told in this way splits into two wings, the beautiful and the beneficial. The beautiful is the brilliant operation involving surrounding Ukraine's army while it is engaged in a foreign land. The beneficial is freeing the Ukrainian nation from a bloodsucking fascist junta. (The most dangerous metaphor in this Russian text is the mention of the word 'denazification'. After the Russian-impelled Nuremberg, it could mean anything.)

As it was in Ukraine in 1918, so it was for people in Transcaucasia, Central Europe, Afghanistan, Latin America, Africa and elsewhere, whose histories Russia strove to rewrite for the rest of the world. Soon the greatest temptation will appear, to make Ukraine the way you imagined it would be. Someone will appear – as old Corleone taught us – who'll propose a convenient solution: as it was with the Western Ukrainian National Republic. And this will be someone we see as being one of ours.

The call to pray for our government, and for all those engaged in the service and protection of our country, is as meaningful now as ever. We must be careful, however. There are already lots of saboteurs around. But writing history is, thankfully, like a tennis match in some ways. One writes while another edits.

Translated by Mark Andryczyk

And Everything Comes True

Yuri Andrukhovych

4 March 2022

It was 2009 and Berlin, as one of Europe's leading capital cities, had already begun marking the twentieth anniversary of the crumbling of the Wall, of Europe becoming united. The Berlin Academy of Arts invited me to write a text and read it on stage. I wrote an essay called 'And Nonetheless, a Wall'. I didn't want to match the joyful tone of the other presentations. It began: 'I cannot agree with the idea that the unification of Europe, its East with its West, so beautifully begun twenty years ago, has, first, been done successfully, and second, that it has been done at all. I don't believe that today, on this anniversary year, we can say that "New Europe" is a historic success. There is something else, too, that prevents me feeling celebratory, along with the global economic crisis.'

It was the thought of Ukraine, where the Wall had not yet fallen. A few punctures had started to appear, but we remained on the worst side of it. The year 2009 brought the final decline of the Orange Revolution drive, countless fractures and betrayals in the pro-European camp, a progressively more heated war of mutual destruction between Mr Yushchenko and Mrs Tymoshenko, the increasingly blatant insolence of the pro-Moscow opposition, and several other nasty events.*

The attitude of Europeans, both the elites and the common people, towards us was diminishing right in front of our eyes, heading towards rock bottom at ever-increasing speed. The Second Gas Dispute had just concluded with the signing of prohibitive and shameful accords in Moscow.† Europe saw Ukraine as weak, divided and hopeless. The Orange beauty of the Maidan no longer stirred anyone. It ceased to be taken seriously.

Russia was instead forgiven for everything, from war, partition and annexation in Georgia to dishonourably and cynically intimidating Ukraine with threats around gas. All this shit is Russia getting what it wanted, both from Europe and from us. As the Russians say – *Vsio pazvolieno!* Everything is permissible!

My essay was bitter. But I didn't delude myself that it would be influential in any way. The Academy of Arts, although an

---

* The Orange Revolution was a series of protests that took place in Ukraine between November 2004 and January 2005. Demonstrators were contesting the legitimacy, due to voter fraud and corruption, of the country's 2004 presidential elections, when it was announced that Viktor Yanukovych had defeated his opponent Viktor Yushchenko. The results were eventually overturned in court and Yushchenko won the re-vote. Yulia Tymoshenko co-led the revolution with Yushchenko and was appointed by him as Ukraine's prime minister after the Orange victory. In time the two developed a bitter feud that severely crippled the revolution's reformist and democratic ideals. The Orange Revolution protests were centred on Kyiv's Independence Square (Maidan Nezalezhnosty), also the site of Ukraine's 2013–14 Revolution of Dignity.

† In 2009 Yulia Tymoshenko, now prime minister of Ukraine, pressured by Russia's threats to leave Europe without energy, rushed through the signing of a gas deal with the then Russian prime minister Vladimir Putin that was detrimental for Ukraine.

important intellectual and cultural forum, was fairly irrelevant within Germany's Realpolitik. But I needed to express my bitterness, to spoil this inappropriate celebration, at least a little.

I concluded: 'Yet again I have abandoned any optimism. But I will not stop stubbornly repeating my favourite argument: Europe will have to open itself to Ukraine. That may be hard to imagine, considering the state of Ukraine and the state of Europe today. But on its "path to freedom, where the people of Europe await it", Ukraine today is still basically where it was ten years ago, at the end of the 1990s. Let's be honest: it's in the grey zone, like in early post-Soviet times, lacking any prospects. But I am sure we will be together. Europe is fated to become united. There is one, certain guarantor of this: Russia. Our big, strong, dear north-eastern brother and neighbour will do everything necessary to make this happen. The only question is what price will be paid for it over the decade to come.'

People actually applauded. I surmise that few from an audience of such brilliant intelligence recognized my sarcasm concerning our 'dear north-eastern brother'. I don't know how my final sentence regarding the price was understood, and by whom. I meant the highest of all possible prices: countless Ukrainian lives, ruining, burning, cultural and natural catastrophes, all those things that those war criminals from the Russian Federation have brought to us now, exactly thirteen years after I wrote my essay. Exactly thirteen; the date that file was created was 6 March 2009.

Well, Russia did indeed fulfil that prediction. Not entirely within the next decade, as I had written, but in the following one. Although, if we remember that Russia started this war back in 2014, then indeed it was within a decade.

And what about Europe? Has it responded as I had hoped it would, for so many years?

Yes, Europe opened up, at its borders, for our refugees. At least there is that, for now.

But all those massive blue-yellow decorations, all that admiration and empathy, all the standing ovations and gatherings of thousands of people in the centre of that same Berlin or in tens of other capitals, are no longer enough. It's all very moving, and wonderful, but it is no longer enough. Our children, our mothers and fathers, our old and young, are perishing. Every day, every night and every hour. Our country is dying, our cities, bridges, buildings, airports and monuments are disappearing.

Now we need something much larger than prayers and tears. Kindness and generosity are not enough, nor is warmth or words of support. We need fearless action. Europe, don't be afraid! Become great, stand up and fight, tear down this Wall.

Translated by Mark Andryczyk

Run Away

Olena Huseinova

17 March 2022

I found Uwe Timm during my night shift. My night shift starts at 9 p.m. and finishes at 9 a.m. Twelve hours at the microphone. Ukrainian Radio has been like this since 24 February. The broadcast no longer gets interrupted, the night isn't filled with repeated airings of earlier daytime programmes. The night is filled with news from our television colleagues and with our voices. And I can speak to people who weren't able to catch my show before, who live in the US or Canada, whose night is my day and whose day is my night. I now work from 9 p.m. to 9 a.m. and write invitations emphasizing that 'I can call whenever it would be convenient for you.' Over the past week I've managed to speak to Marko Robert Stech about Displaced Persons' camps and Alexander Motyl about the collapse of Russia.* But even a convenient time may turn out to be inconvenient. Today I didn't manage to find someone to speak to on the other side of the ocean. But I found Uwe Timm. A boring article from the Ukrainian

* 200,000 Ukrainians lived in Displaced Persons' camps in American, French and British zones in post-WWII Germany and Austria. Marko Robert Stech is a Ukrainian-Canadian scholar and writer. Alexander J. Motyl is a Ukrainian-American scholar and writer.

9

Academy of Sciences' journal, scanned and tossed into the internet, mentioned two books, one about Hamburg during Germany's capitulation and the other an autobiographical reconstruction of the story of a brother who died on the shores of the Dnipro river, and who was a member of the SS Panzer Division *Totenkopf* (Death's Head), the same unit that controlled the concentration-camp system, and that, according to a historical encyclopedia, also handled other functions during the occupation. I download both Timm books and begin reading them. Their plots are intertwined: Hamburg in the days before capitulation, bombed-out buildings, random things salvaged from them, the search for news and gossip. These are all things that my friends in Kharkiv, Sumy and the Kyiv region can also talk about. That is why I sought out Uwe Timm. So that the written and real worlds could hold together. To assure myself that all of this has happened before, that it has all been written about in books.

However, the reading stops. Uwe Timm mentions the fairy tale of Bluebeard. This tale is often used in stories whenever there is a need for a metaphor for domestic abuse or dangerous silence. Uwe Timm uses it too. Uwe Timm writes about a box lying in front of him containing the personal possessions of his brother, the SS officer, which had been sent to him by his parents directly from the hospital in Ukraine. He is afraid to open it because it includes a diary which may contain horrific things, and Uwe Timm is ashamed of what he might find. Uwe Timm is afraid of reading the diary even though he knows that his brother served in one of the first three units of the SS, the *Totenkopf* Division, that took part in combat, not occupying, activity. Uwe Timm is scared, he knows what the SS did on the shores of the Dnipro river, but he doesn't yet know whether his brother did those things. And while the box

remains closed he can simply remain afraid, instead of decid-
ing what to do with the unknown. Thus, Uwe Timm is afraid.
He recalls that he was also afraid of the fairy tale of Bluebeard
when his mother read it to him. The moment the young wife
inserts the little key in the door of the forbidden room. Uwe
Timm repeats this several times. Bluebeard's room is as
terrifying as the box with the things belonging to his brother,
the SS man. It's like his diary in that box. And I stop. I can't
read on.

I was never scared of the story of Bluebeard. I sympathized
with Bluebeard. Because it's easy to sympathize with someone when you don't know the things they've done. I knew
nothing about Bluebeard's dead wives and about the rivers of
blood in the forbidden room. My mother edited this fairy tale
when she read it to me. She cut this sentence out: 'The sisters
also feared him because he had been married many times in
the past, but no one knew where his previous wives had disappeared to.' And that room, where the bodies of those wives
and the rivers of blood were, in my mother's version, was
empty, and the key simply fell to the floor, in the dirt. I guess
that's probably often the case for those who only listen. For
those who trust every word. For those who miss the very
beginning (and that sentence about the missing wives is the
tale's second). For me that fairy tale was about unfair losses.
Bluebeard lets his young wife into his home, shares all of his
great and small things, all of his silver and gold, all his old and
new objects, which probably took him a long time to assemble.
And basically gives her all the keys to all the doors of his building. 'Open everything that you want,' he says. 'Go wherever
you want.' Except for 'the small room', he says. For me he is
just a man with a blue beard who has enormous wealth and
generosity but doesn't have several missing wives. Only one

wife, who snuck into the little room and damaged the key. She summons her heavily armed brothers and they fly in on white horses, kill Bluebeard and move into his home, walk along his carpets, command his servants and harness his horses to coaches. And as the last sentence, which my mother did not cut out, says – they didn't even mention him. They don't mention the secret room either. It fades from the text.

I first saw that second sentence and found out about Bluebeard's missing and dead wives when I came to read Angela Carter and Clarissa Pinkola Estés. I ended up having to read the fairy tale on my own. So now I know about Bluebeard's dead wives. Although I don't understand how the first one got into that little room. If Bluebeard killed his wives because they looked into that little room and saw the dead wives, then what did the first wife see? Carter and Estés convince me that the little room is amazing. It's full of wonders created especially for me. It's just that they had been hidden from me and now I need to rebel, to overcome my superstitions and enter that little room. And then, I guess, run up to the tallest tower of Bluebeard's building and call for the brothers on white horses or dragoons and musketeers, like in the first iteration of the tale.

My night shift continues. I walk out into the corridor and see a white window. In early March dawn comes at 4:30 a.m. I look out of the window and forget about the second sentence of Bluebeard's tale. I think about the brothers on white horses, dragoons and musketeers, who, without pause, rush his beautiful building with its rugs, goblets, carriages and horses. And I look at the brightening March sky and shout up to it, to Bluebeard: 'Run away!' Of all your dear things, grab the first you come across. Like Uwe Timm's parents during *Operation Gomorrah*, when their four-storey building caught fire: a smoking table, a few towels, a duvet, two porcelain statuettes, one porcelain plate and a suitcase, which they thought contained valuable things but that turned out to be filled with old Christmas ornaments. I know that Bluebeard will not manage to escape. I know that for many, many years Uwe Timm's parents, at Christmas tables, during card games, drinking wine, smoking cigars, will not talk about how they might have prevented their older sons from becoming members of the SS and spared them from death on the shores of the Dnipro but will, instead, look for reasons why victory failed. They'll replay battles, give directives, shuffle generals, and even remove Hitler from command of the army. I continue looking out of the window and, in my thoughts, transfer Operation Gomorrah 2,106.59 kilometres east. I imagine what parents of a young man who at this moment is dying somewhere on the shores of the Moshchunka river are grabbing to take with them. I toss Bluebeard into the village of Moshchun itself. He stands in his house, looks out as the March sky dawns; he can still escape. My next night shift is in two days. I will not continue reading Uwe Timm. Let him find the guts to open the box of his SS-member brother, who died on the shores of the Dnipro, without me. I'll download *The Walking Dead*, where there is no doubt about who you should sympathize with, who you should fear, and when to yell 'Run away!'

Translated by Mark Andryczyk

Ashamed

Olena Huseinova

30 March 2022

Everyone in Lviv knew Torobi, even though he only arrived on 26 February. Everyone knew him and everyone loved him. Even when they realized that wine could also be purchased in Sokilnyky. And even when the ban on alcohol consumption no longer considered wine to be dangerous. One could procure wine from Torobi. Not purchase it, because Torobi never sold his stash of red and rosé. This was not because he was wary of the ban on alcohol. Wine could be obtained from Torobi by means of exchange. For the phone number of a good hair stylist or dentist, for a car ride, for a spring coat, for a dinner invitation, for an offer to stroll through Stryiskyi Park, for anything that could make one recall that, at one time, life seemed boring and mundane. The first exchange for a bottle was made by me. We met up in one of those Lviv restaurants which, just a half a year ago, we tried not to visit because nobody wanted to sit in a basement. The name of the restaurant was Beirut and it served seven types of hummus. I went in with the foolhardy plan of attempting to order some wine. My plans to get my hands on some wine during the ban on alcohol were limited to bootlegging schemes lifted straight out of lowbrow gangster movies. This basement restaurant was the perfect place for bootleggers. Then I saw Torobi, who was trying to convince the waitress that it was a bad idea to close the kitchen at 5 p.m. The waitress was holding a credit-card terminal in one hand and an empty bottle with a wide neck, for tap water, in the other. I understood that it was futile to ask for wine in Beruit, where at 5 p.m. you couldn't even get one of those seven types of hummus. Even if you were to talk like you were in a bad movie and say something like 'Listen honey, just pour some white right into this bottle and we'll just say it's water with lemon'. Air-raid alarms then forced the waitress to keep us in the basement and treat us to plain hummus. We sat at the only free table. The waitress brought some lavash and deep plates of hummus, drizzled with a generous amount of olive oil and sprinkled with chickpeas.

Torobi tore off a piece of lavash and scooped up some hummus.

'Not bad, but the name "hummus" sucks,' he said, 'I would call it "chick paste". They should serve it in those half-circle containers that come with a cover and let you eat it with your fingers. Or a teaspoon.'

Well, this sure isn't Reiterska,* I thought to myself. We chewed in silence. I, who had come looking for wine, not hummus, and Torobi, about whom I knew nothing. Perhaps like everyone else he was hiding out from the war, from patrols bringing blank forms in which your last name, first name and patronymic, your date of birth, your passport number and its place of issue are entered, and which urgently recommend that you show up at the enlistment office, the address of which can be found on the website. March had not yet begun, and it seemed to all of us that we were not afraid of death since we

---

* Reiterska is the name of a street in Ukraine's capital, Kyiv, which features several hip cafés with diverse food options.

no longer felt like we were alive. In our heads we assembled lists of unfinished business, things left behind. We planned on learning how to drive a stick shift, on going to the shooting range, and looking up how artillery works on YouTube. But we did none of this. Instead, we searched for wine and hoped to share it with our friends. Torobi came to Lviv from Kyiv. He escaped like I did.

'How did you get here?' I asked Torobi.

A classic conversation between escapees. There were two possible ways to escape, by car or by train. There were also two stories, one about village roads which had never experienced such traffic, and another about trains stormed by passengers. And there were also stories about things and habits left behind. Every time we shared them with one another we were overjoyed by the similarities in our stories, even down to the tiniest details. We wanted to feel that burning shamefulness, that there was nothing we hid from each other, that we knew everything about one another. I came by car and my story was about village roads and about a random box of my grandma's Czech crystal wine glasses, which, on 24 February, I was supposed to take over to Karyna, who would buy junk and sell it on Instagram.

'I came in a baggage van,' Torobi told me.

I wasn't surprised. I'd even seen scooters on the road. That was also inconvenient and shameful.

'Refrigerator Class A,' Torobi added.

I wanted to say that it didn't matter, everyone came however they could and there was no need to make excuses. That is, you needed to make excuses for why you escaped, but not for how you did it. However, Torobi quickly added: 'But my wife, son and cat stayed behind. Well, my former wife, and her son. The cat too.'

I was beginning to feel uncomfortable. Having found this out, I didn't have something like 'Forget about it' or 'It's fine' to say, after which we could continue to eat hummus in silence, washed down with tap water.

'It would have been too cold for them in the refrigerator car,' Torobi continued, as he set aside the lavash and the hummus and looked at me carefully.

I need to get up and leave, I thought. Screw the air alarms.

'Don't be scared,' Torobi said, 'there are no dead bodies there; +12°C does not work for dead bodies. My life is there. I trade wine.'

I guess chance lucky meetings do exist, I thought. To escape from Kyiv, where the Russian armies are approaching, get stuck in a Lviv basement hummus joint in the middle of an air alarm during the alcohol ban, and meet a crazy wine wheeler-dealer.

'By February 23rd the wine was ready. I'm completely sorted out! I've got corrugated boxes, fasteners and pallets. And neither the temperature nor the sun's rays get in there, no matter where you're parked.'

I didn't care what it was made of, I thought, and counted the cash, asking whether Torobi would be OK with euros. I imagined that I would return to our improvised shelter with a case of wine. I imagined how happy Lina and Alia would be. We could invite Liokha and Kristina and Sofiika, who had let us live in the office, and Ihor, who gave us all of his mattress pads and sleeping bags, and Taras, in whose jeans and sweater I now sat. And we'd get the Czech crystal from the trunk.

'But I won't sell it. I am ashamed.'

And he told me how a year ago he'd sold his car and his apartment and gone to live with his former wife, her son and cat, bought a baggage van-refrigerator, found an Austrian winery, ordered 400 litres of red and 400 litres of rosé (because he didn't like white), how this wine was poured into bottles in Transcarpathia, and how he himself came up with a super-cool label. And then, on 23 February, the wine was ready.

And then war arrived.

'What kind of wine?' I asked.

'Zweigel,' Torobi said.

His refrigerator was on Pasichna St. Torobi pulled out a box, and from it a bottle, and offered it to me.

I shone my phone on the label. Against a red background I saw a big letter Z.

A week later, Torobi's former wife was living with us in the shelter, with her son and their cat.

Translated by Mark Andryczyk

War Diary: The Fifth Week of a Long February

Olena Stiazhkina

7 April 2022

Kyiv, 23 March 2022

The little man is the alpha and omega of so-called Great Russian Culture. Small, pathetic, cowardly, patient, grey, voiceless. Wherever and whoever they are, they have no ability to act.

The powerful mute Gerasim* humbly drowns the only soul who loves him. He looks into the eyes of his dog and throws a rope with a stone around its neck. He kills it, betrays it. He could've sold it or given it away. He could've tied it up in the woods and visited it every day, fed it and loved it. But Gerasim is a little man. He is too weak to resist his circumstances, but strong enough to kill.

The trembling creature Raskolnikov tests his power through murder. He is curious. He is a little man who believes that to become great means destroying another.

The little man is an unknown soldier, a nameless hero, a missing warrior. They are innumerable. They have no name:

---

* Gerasim is the hero of Ivan Turgenev's story 'Mumu' (1854) about a deaf and mute serf whose life of poverty is brought into sharp relief by his connection with Mumu, a dog he rescues and then drowns at the order of his landlady.

they are merged into a single body of a machine that either devours or kills.

For decades Great Russian Culture has been inviting the world to cry for those who shudder with fear, uncertainty and powerlessness, who commit crimes they can't resist.

When the war started the people who own the apartment my elder family members rent called and said: 'You know, with things the way they are, just pay the utility bills if you can. No need to pay the rent. We are good people.'

Before the war I would not have called them good. They, the mother and the daughter, were kind of spineless. There were a lot of spineless people in Kyiv then. They thought what was done by Moscovia in 2014 fitted into the scheme of 'not everything is so clearcut'; that 'we are still fraternal peoples'; 'we can't have any influence'. I don't know whether their views have changed now that those 'brotherly people' are skinning people alive out of curiosity and powerlessness. I believe they have.

But even if they haven't, they called to show what kind of people they are. Between the little, who cannot decide anything, and the good, who are capable of doing something, they chose the good.

Throughout the war I have been taking crime shows on TV instead of sleeping pills. They're about special forces, police stations, private detectives, and so on. They lull me to sleep and assure me that good triumphs over evil. They let me believe that the worst maniacs put down their weapons; the filthiest scum cooperates with the investigation; the most corrupt policemen confess to treason and shield their own from bullets in order to remain, at least in small part, a good person.

This is the question, the key question that comes up time

and again when negotiating with criminals: 'Are you a good person?' It's a different mirror for civilization to look into. Not the nameless soldier, but Private Ryan, who must be saved because he is his mother's last son.

'Am I a good person?' is asked by teenagers and older people, the rich and poor, men and women. Moreover, even the zombies in apocalyptic films prefer to say, 'I am a good person', and then refuse to bite a child.

This is the difference. This is the war between the little and the good, between the ruthless, cruel, brainless, shameless, dirty little ones and the good ones. If the civilization built on the question of being a good person loses, Gerasim will systematically drown dogs, and Raskolnikov will methodically kill the elderly. The Z-swastika of the Great Russian Culture will leave nothing human. Nowhere. White Fang will never find his Weedon Scott and Private Ryan will be buried in a mass grave.

Kyiv, 24 March 2022

'I'd love a sweet, but I won't have one'; 'It doesn't hurt so much that I should go to hospital'; 'Don't take water for yourself, they need it'; 'How can I rest? They won't be able to cope without me.'

It's not as horrible here as it is there. We are not in a trench. My relatives are safe. We have electricity. Shops are open.

All my friends and acquaintances often (to be honest, constantly) talk about feeling deep shame. They are ashamed to be alive when our people are dying, to eat when they are starving, ashamed to want something trivial when so many couldn't even think to want it.

Psychologists call it guilt or survivor's shame. Whatever . . . Not necessarily. Because, as of now, we are survivors. In this moment, when I am writing this.

We are not in a trench, and we have electricity, for the time being. However, it is interesting that those who are defending us on the front lines also sometimes (hopefully not all the time) feel ashamed: for not doing something well enough, for not being in combat, for being alive, for not being able to do more.

I am not thinking about the mental health of people in a large-scale war with cannibals.

I am thinking about them. About the cannibals, who have formulated the slogan: 'I am not ashamed', an ancestral simulacrum.

Fucking hell. Our country is choking with guilt from all that is unfinished and has come undone. The hashtag 'I'm not ashamed' sticks out of hell's abyss.

They are not ashamed to kill, loot, rape or wet their pants when they are captured. They are not ashamed of missiles and bombs being aimed at civilians. They are not ashamed to wear a fur coat stolen from an apartment where a family was probably killed. They are not ashamed to lie, they are not ashamed to curse, they are not ashamed to threaten the world with a bare ass topped with a nuclear button.

Finally, I can now understand why.

Feelings of shame and guilt are a result of the brain's ability to process complex feelings. Do cats and dogs feel shame? With cats it is clear that everything in the house belongs to the cat, and it is the two-legged slave who should feel shame. It is more complicated with dogs. It is believed that they don't really feel guilty but instead sometimes pretend to be ashamed. At least dogs can pretend.

These people cannot. In the world around us, shame is completely alien to the flora. It is partly present in the fauna, useful and useless minerals, as well as in any human work. A stone, a rose and a tank are not ashamed. Can a Russian be a rose? Obviously not.

Their boasts about how they don't feel shame are connected with what Prince Sviatoslav of Kyiv once emphasized (or is believed to have emphasized): 'The dead have no shame.' However, the context of the prince was heroic, not shitty, as in this case.

But the thought is good.

They are not ashamed, because they are dead.

Dead.

So, the Ukrainian army protects us all and reduces word and deed to one denominator. If you, I-am-not-ashamed one, are dead, then you should be at the cemetery of Russian warships.

Kyiv, 25 March 2022

If one day, or better two, passes without massive bombing attacks on civilians and with a small victory in several directions at once, we immediately become political opponents. No, no, we keep loading, cleaning, transporting, arranging, counting, everything is OK here. However, on these days we load and clean in mute dissatisfaction with each other. On bright days, which the sun of victory seems to be, we know for sure that those who are against us voted for the wrong people.

We count and carry in silence, full of confrontation and the desire to say something very straightforward.

In an air raid, in the moment of sorrow from the east, from

the south, sorrow that is now everywhere, rage instantly returns, along with the solidarity rage brings. 'We are not fighting for the shit we have elected (or not elected). We are fighting here for Ukraine. Let all the sons of Russofascist bitches be cursed.'

My dear friend spends every night in the vestibule of a nine-storey building. The area where she lives is often hit. Her neighbours are with her, a young couple. As a rule, they knock on her door to make sure she does not miss the siren. She can. She is a historian. When she goes into a research frenzy, she can even forget her own name. She has a joke about this: 'Tell me, please, what's your name?' – 'Is it urgent?'

For a month and one day she has been spending nights in the vestibule. Every now and then she comes out with: 'May they rot in hell!' In the first few days, her words either pierced the silence or merged with the sound of rockets and planes. My friend does not like silence or inattention to her words. Now the trained neighbours know that there must always be a response. 'May they rot in hell!' my dear friend says. 'In agony!' the young couple answers her loudly in unison.

To the list of why the world needs the UN, IAEA* and OSCE[†] I add the Red Cross.

On the thirtieth day of the war, does the Red Cross still have a special operation?

There is every reason to believe that soon its headquarters will be seen in the Kremlin. Somewhere near the OSCE.

---

* International Atomic Energy Agency.
† Organization for Security and Co-operation in Europe.

In the occupied cities the Gauleiters* and their henchmen have lists of Ukrainian activists. The latter are taken away somewhere and abducted, tortured. They are shot execution style.

Moscovia has long been preparing for a final offensive. Their lists were expanded and supplemented with ATO† participants, soldiers of the armed forces, party leaders. Of course, these lists were not created in the Kremlin. Along with those who want to live in a free country, there are always those who do not want to live in any country. We also have the dead from birth. However, the fact that Judas was with Christ does not cancel Christianity.

To the stupid Russian question 'Where have you been for eight years?' I have an answer: where I am now. Because to be in Donetsk since 2014 meant to turn into a 'victim of the Kyiv Nazis' at any moment, being shelled by the 'liberators' themselves to create a convincing picture for Rusofascist TV. Sergei Loznitsa has a movie‡ about this. There is a movie, but there is no position. Because 'peace for the world' in our case means 'a world without Ukraine'.

Kyiv, 26 March 2022

Coffee shops, bakeries and small markets are open in Kyiv. Everything you need from the territorial defence list can be

---

* The name for Russian propagandists and collaborationist officials, which comes from the German name for regional leaders of the Nazi Party.
† Anti-Terrorist Operation Zone, the area where Ukrainian forces have been fighting against Russian separatists in Eastern Ukraine since the Russian annexation in 2014.
‡ Sergei Loznitsa's 2018 movie *Donbass*.

bought in a supermarket. But we stop at every open window saying 'coffee' and at street vendors. I endure it. Coffee can be suspended, sausage and sauerkraut can be added to the delicacies on the list. If you don't stop in time, you'll only get half a tub of sauerkraut. And even less sausage, a little less than ten kilograms.

But stopping around the bakery, which smells of buttery pastries, breaks my patience. 'No!' I shout. 'No pastry!'

A wind that blows in the right direction cannot be stopped.

He comes out of the shop with a box of buns. Before the war they were called cinnamon buns. To eat them on the street you need napkins, both wet and dry, and plates, or at least some paper to hold the delicious food in your hands, too. One bite of a cinnamon bun is too big for the mouth.

'I can't eat that much!'

'This is not for you! This is in addition to the list.'

'Another addition, some of them have already bought the Napoleon torte.'

'So what? Have they seized Moscow?'

'No, the commander said that, as of now, the Napoleon torte and other pastries are not welcome. Pastries give you gas, OK?'

'Let's take them to the hospital.'

I'm looking at him from a dietary perspective.

'If we can't take them to the hospital, let's give them away. We'll stand here and distribute them, like Santa Claus.'

'Santa!' I shout. People on the street look at me with understanding. These days everyone is going crazy any way they want. But not me. 'Santa Claus, rather than that bastard Russian Father Frost! May he croak in hell!'

Passers-by smile. They're on my side.

'All right, all right,' the defeated man whines. 'Then let's make crackers out of them. One bag or two?'

'Why did you buy them in the first place?'

'The economy, Lyonya, the economy. Someone has to support it. As long as there's money, it'll be me.'

'Then you can have some crackers.'

Today was sunny, windy, rainy and cold. It's February again. The same February as thirty-two days ago.

Kyiv, 27 March 2022

The day Victory arrives someone will have to speak. It will not be me. I do not want to, and I won't be able to. I want quiet, to hear the wind, to hear the grass, to hear the predatory steps of the cat in the yard. Not my voice, not your voice, not anybody's voice. Quiet. So that words and sounds do not interrupt 'that which is not dying'.

But someone must speak. It will be the same sacred duty as being at the front, volunteering, hospitals. Through speeches, interviews, reports, those who can speak will give others the opportunity to hear whispers of those who have left.

To hear a whisper, to smell, taste, the cold or warmth of your palms. They will be somewhere here, mixed with the air, leaves, water, perfume, gasoline, coffee, Easter bread. Somewhere where my ear will be, which does not hear and is not going to hear anything but them.

It won't be a dream, although it'll be as if I am dreaming. I want it to be a miracle. I want it to be everywhere, so everyone can recognize it. A miracle in which some rounded 'r' will reverberate, or a stutter, with the tone of an opera singer, tenor, soprano, bass.

In our silence we will recognize their voices and our clenched jaws will open and perhaps let out some words. Or maybe not. I do not want to speak and will not speak. I will search, wait and listen. Until I find them, I will not speak.

Kyiv, 28 March 2022

Serhii is four years old. He lives with his grandmother on the eighth floor. When the air-raid siren goes off, Serhii rushes up the stairs and knocks on the doors of every landing with a cheerful shout: 'Ladies and gentlemen! To the shelter, urgently!'

But there is no shelter as such, not a bomb shelter or a basement. People gather on the ground floor and take out chairs, armchairs and sleeping bags in case the siren goes on for a long time.

Ten minutes later, Serhii addresses everyone: 'Tell me, please, does anyone have some fruit drink at home? For a good and polite guest like myself?'

Two or three apartments have some. Serhii tastes each one. He praises the hostesses, hinting that his grandmother 'never knows how to make it like that'. Time goes by.

The 'untrained grandmother' is joined by the grandfather, who 'caught the saboteur and took him as a bribe to the military commissariat'.

Then little Serhii says: 'Does anyone have any bread with honey for a polite guest?' He is cunning. In fact, he does not want bread with honey and counts on the fact that his neighbours do not have a prepared sandwich in their apartments, so he is waiting for biscuits, sweets, chocolate – something forbidden in peacetime.

He says: 'Granny, when we're all killed, who's going to need my beautiful teeth and the healthy food inside my belly?'

He mispronounces a few letters. But the meaning is clear.

Those who have reached the village write that the storks have returned. Those who are waiting for their relatives from Mariupol write that Kadyrov* is there.

We live through the war in different ways, but we will live through Victory in the same way.

The thirty-third day of February. As a child I was told that February is the shortest month.

Many mayors have invested lots of money in their election campaigns. Needless to say, being mayor in Ukraine has always meant being given access to the state budget, out of which they bite a good chunk. They bite off enough for a house in Spain and a little more as an inheritance for their children and grandchildren. And for a beautiful life for themselves.

Now it turns out that the mayors were investing big money to become heroes. And sometimes even martyrs, shot by the enemy for their loyalty to Ukraine.

No one knows where and when the power to be a human being is born. Now it turns out that it is born from everything.

Kyiv, 29 March 2022

There is a deafening noise in the air. The windows do not shudder. Bang-bang-bang. That means it's from us. It means that there is no need to fall on the asphalt and cover your head

---

* The Chechen strongman Ramzan Kadyrov, who sends Chechen troops in support of Putin's army into Ukraine.

with your hands. You can go on. Just a deafening noise in the air. We've got used to it.

There was less noise in Donetsk. However, more targets were hit. In 2014 there were people in Donetsk who went down to the basement at the beginning of summer and came out at the beginning of winter. Now there are people doing this in Kharkiv, Chernihiv and Sumy. In Kyiv, as of now, there are none.

Last night the historian Serhii Kot died of a heart attack. He devoted his life to collecting the cultural heritage looted from Ukraine during the wars and bringing it home. Mr Kot cared about restitution with all his heart. Now his heart has stopped.

My friend Serhii Vaganov writes: 'The city of Mariupol has turned into a topographic map.'

We will not call our war *patriotic*. Patriotism is a Russian military myth from which the Russian form of Nazism has grown. The words *Third Reich* were nothing but a historical allusion, but then there was nothing but shame and blood.

We are fighting for our homeland. Not for the homeland as a symbol, but for people and their freedom. A pro-human war? A human war? A war for independence? And from there, will it be the Hundred Years' War? David's war? The Eight Years' War? A Fierce War? A War of Vengeance? A Victorious War? Can a war have such a name?

Kyiv, 30 March 2022

Someone suggested counting the days by Thursdays, because the war will carry on and counting days will punch you in the gut; the stretch of time is insidiously long. Counting Thursdays is not as painful. Tomorrow, for example, is only the fifth Thursday.

Between the second and third Thursday I found the sky. Between the third and fourth I noticed the air. Before the fifth I had seen the streets. In Kyiv, like other cities where war is on the outskirts and you can leave and arrive by train, not by humanitarian corridor, there are billboards on both sides of the roads.

From the time before the war they display adverts for children's swimming classes and for a concert of Shufutinsky, who looks like a dead Kobzon.

The ones from the war say 'Glory to Mariupol!'; 'Chernihiv, thank you!'; 'On February 24 at 5 a.m., Russia bombed Kyiv'; 'Russian warship, go fuck yourself'; 'Russian soldiers, being alive as a POW is better than being dead in a ditch.'

Most of all I like 'Ministry of Defence. 4.5.0.'

In the language of the military 4.5.0. means 'Everything is fine, everything is calm.'

Everything is calm. Our morning roll call is getting shorter and now consists of three numbers and three periods – 4.5.0.

It's 4.5.0. in Kyiv between the fourth and fifth Thursday.

Calm is not quiet. Our artillery keeps hitting. We say: 'It's working.'

It's working so that we aren't denazified to death by Russian missiles flying from the direction of Bucha, which is nearly destroyed. After all, it was here, during the shelling of Kyiv, that the 'liberators' ate a Central Asian Shepherd dog and boasted about it. Their friends approved. If the next time they are fed up with dry rations, they eat their friend, he will also approve. The friend is not Putin. He is the Russian people, who kill, rape, steal and now eat a Central Asian Shepherd.

*

33

I see the streets. I feel the taste of concrete in my mouth constantly. I have never eaten concrete or even licked it. But I taste concrete.

It turns out hatred can taste different. Today it's concrete. Yesterday it was ashes.

The Russian world is all the flavours of hell.

My ear hurts. A bit less now, but still. The doctor said that it could be worse, but it will get better. I asked: 'Are you from the Donetsk or the Luhansk region?'

'Donetsk,' he replied.

'You're having the same experience now all over again.'

'I wouldn't say so. We were luckier. Only some mortar shells, grads* and tornadoes. And now, what a damn invasion!'

We need a German or a Frenchman to come here. We could start with Macron.

The doctor and I would teach him that grads, tornadoes and mortars are about luck.

We have some marijuana in our apartment. Just a tiny bit, not even enough for one joint. Besides, Mr Policeman, I don't remember where it came from, honestly.

And – just in case – I am in favour of legalizing it for medical purposes.

Once my husband used to hide (keep?) it in the bathroom cabinet. Then somewhere else.

I swear, I don't know where it is now.

Today it turned out that our seventeen-year-old son found it

---

* Multiple-launch rocket systems produced in the USSR and still used by Russia in its war against Ukraine. The Grad system is also called the Hail system in English, which is a direct translation of the word 'grad'.

and took a picture of it with his cellphone so he could shame us in the future.

The future has come. I found my son's cigarettes, even though he swore last year not to smoke again.

I raised an honest citizen. My son had a trump card.

'First, those cigarettes are from last year, I kept them as a reminder. Second, people who hide marijuana in the bathroom should mind their own business.'

'I don't know anything about it. It's not ours. It's not us. And there's nothing in there at all.'

'There wasn't?' he asks, sternly and sadly. After a pause, burning me with his eyes, he says: 'You know, Mum, I understand that you are embarrassed. But let's never joke like they do in the "Russian world . . ."'

Kyiv, 31 March 2022

Hair salons have opened. Not all of them, only barbershops have opened. Kyiv wants to cut men's hair first. The girls who cut off their braids to go to the front will gradually grow their hair back, for themselves and for others.

Prices in the barbershops are flexible. For soldiers it's free of charge, for volunteers it's possibly free, but if you have money, then pay as much as you have, that's what the price is. For everyone else there are three options: 400, 600 or 800 hryvnias. Half of everything goes to the Armed Forces of Ukraine.

When women's hairdressers open I will cut my hair by one centimetre each week. Half for the Armed Forces, half to support the economy. My hair is forty centimetres long and I believe that I won't be bald before our Victory.

*

Geography is painful. Understudied and forgotten, it has been so long since school and the geography of Ukraine was painful.

Instead of the marks of minerals, rivers, lakes, ravines, steppes and forests, there are now the bloody marks of missiles or bombs.

Every city, village and town's name is engraved deeply enough in memory that it will be painful for decades to come.

They say that wounds will be cured and scars will heal.

But they won't. They just won't be visible; you won't be able to touch them or run your hands over them.

Remaining inside, they will be tugged invisibly by big reminders and small flashes of memory.

For years I have been carrying the keys to my apartment in Donetsk in my bag. I no longer remember which key opens which lock. I forget, I forgot.

When I happen to touch them (the size of my bag allows me to consider it both an emergency escape-bag and a burial place for the corpses of enemies) I feel black blood flowing inside, in invisible and perhaps non-existent parts of my body, this blood covers my eyes. But I do not cry. I hate them. I hate them, the Russians. I will hate them until the very end.

All of them.

Translated by Alla Perminova and Michael M. Naydan

About Bullets in the Back of the Head

Yuri Andrukhovych

8 April 2022

The geographical distance from Russia determines the fate of places in Ukraine, along with the fate of their inhabitants. The closer to Russia, the more terrifying it is. The further away, the safer you are. This is how Mykola Khvylovy's* directive 'Away from Moscow!' operates now.

No matter how aware you are of this ever-more-evident rule, it won't get any easier. It reminds me of how twenty years ago I ended one of my poems with: 'In everything else, *this* is simply a song / a long beautiful song about the path to the abyss / or let's say, no less beautiful, / about a bullet in the back of your head.'

From Demianiv Laz,† in the Pasichna suburb of Ivano-Frankivsk, to Bucha, near Kyiv, is about 600 kilometres and

---

* Leading Ukrainian prose writer and essayist Mykola Khvylovy (1893–1933), who led the renaissance of Ukrainian culture in the 1920s that later came to be called the 'Executed Renaissance'. Khvylovy committed suicide before he surely would have been arrested and executed by Stalin's regime. One of Khvylovy's primary calls was for Ukrainian writers to look towards Europe and away from Russia.

† Demianiv Laz is a site near a Jewish cemetery on the outskirts of the city of Ivano-Frankivsk that has been turned into a solemn memorial. The name literally means 'Demian's Path'.

eighty-one years. But these temporal and spatial distances have now collapsed. Crimes springing from the same kind of evil have been committed in both places.

Today there are many refugees in the city, and excursions are organized for them to fill their time with something useful. I don't know if they are taken to Demianiv Laz. It's possible they're not, so as not to further traumatize them. And, probably, this is the right thing to do.

But how can we, then, fully, in historical cyclicality, understand what happened in Bucha? In Borodianka, Irpin, Hostomel, Makariv? This list of names is really much longer. They have only recently stopped just being names and have become wounds. And this list doesn't begin with Demianiv Laz. It goes back much further. It doesn't begin with Zabar, nor with Sandarmos. Perhaps with Baturyn?

Let's return to Demianiv Laz. The echo of which was first heard somewhere at the turn of the 1960s and 1970s. It seems that Radio Liberty – those who risked listening heard it – broadcast that, on the outskirts of modern Frankivsk, Russians (or should we call them Soviets?), beginning in 1939 and especially in the spring of June 1941, executed about five hundred people by firing squad – both those they had already condemned, as well as random people who were seized and taken to be exterminated, particularly women and children. Their remains, the radio reported, were lying somewhere in the ground there. The quote-unquote *competent* authorities reacted to this right away. In an urgent secret meeting it was decided that the landscape should be changed beyond recognition, 'walloping' the wicked place to the max. Soon after, several hectares of a forest were cut down and a spring was filled with garbage. To remove any resemblance to what was there before, artificially made embankments transformed the surface, which had been totally flat, into hills. Such was the political land-art of the time.

Two decades passed and the shovels and Sovs* were beginning to wobble. In September and October 1989 Memorial†
activists, with the aid of local residents, including some surviving witnesses, dug their way down to human bones and skulls riddled with bullet holes. It is said that a representative of the *competent* authorities present at the excavations said: 'You've won.' The bones were found at the very end of the day. If they hadn't found anything that day the authorities would have revoked permission for the searches, and the initiators would have had to stand before a court for provocation and libel.

Thus several weeks of scrupulous work began: the extraction of human remains, half-decayed things, court-ordered medical expertise, and the piecemeal identification of the tortured individuals. The total (I'm afraid it isn't the final count) was 524 human lives. The reason for their deaths was being Ukrainian. Women, children, teenagers, young people. All of them.

The communist authorities scrambled to declare that it was, they said, the work of the Germans. But this explanation didn't stand up for very long. The shape of the holes in the chest negated it completely. In case anyone was lucky and survived by chance, the killers both shot them and made a controlled strike with a bayonet to the chest. The fact that the holes were four-sided and diamond-shaped indicated it was

---

* The word *sovok* means both shovel as well as a derisive word for Soviet people who mindlessly believed in the USSR.
† An NGO founded during Soviet times to promote human rights and to root out and publicize historical atrocities. The organization was shut down in 2021 by the Putin regime.

done by the Soviets. The Germans had no such bayonets; their flat ones were closer to Soviet knife bayonets, used much later.

That Russians tortured peaceful Ukrainians in Bucha, in numbers commensurate with those of the victims of Demianiv Laz (although in neither place is there a final count), is an example of another similarity: holes in the backs of heads. Skulls from Laz and heads from Bucha are proof that the very same *technology* was used. Russian grandfathers passed it on to their grandsons as a testament to a great culture. Russian grandsons proved to be worthy followers. The Russian language has the best word for this – *posledysh* (the youngest runt).

This is an anti-world with its own tradition, anti-humanity with its own ritual. A very acute genetic legacy lies before us, of Demianiv Lazes, of Buchas, from a single chain of deaths.

But there is one difference. In Bucha they wrapped the victims' heads in their own shirts. I could never guess why. Was it like blindfolding the condemned for execution? I happened to come across this explanation from one of *their* (Russian) commentators. Because who else would try to explain it, if not them?

When you shoot someone close up in the back of their head, blood and brain matter splatters all over you. Try washing that off later. That's why they wrapped their heads before shooting them. We will someday discover whether this was done by their own hands, or by the hands of the victims themselves.

Russian grandfathers in 1941 ordered special leather aprons for this task. It is surprising that in 2022 military suppliers did not equip their descendants with something similar. But the descendants had already discovered their own way.

It so happens that the sound of something often reveals its meaning.

About Bullets in the Back of the Head

When Biden called Putin a butcher a few weeks ago, the world didn't yet know the name Bucha. Now the butcher Putin and Bucha will forever echo each other, horrifically.

And the word 'asvabaditeli'* (liberators) is now pronounced by residents of the Kharkiv or Sumy regions with the same intonation as the Galicians.† Only we started to do that in 1939.

Translated by Michael M. Naydan and Alla Perminova

---

* The phonetic pronunciation of the Russian word for 'liberators'.
† Ukrainians from the region of Western Ukraine, which is called Halychyna in Ukrainian and often rendered in English as Galicia. The Galicians experienced this kind of violence in 1939–45 from the Nazi and Soviet armies, which both saw themselves as 'liberators'.

From Vladivostok to Lisbon

Oleksandr Boichenko

12 April 2022

I've quoted this a hundred times, and I'm going to quote it for the hundredth-and-first time, too: in 1958, when French journalists asked the Polish writer Marek Hłasko, 'Is there a way in which we can understand one another better?', he replied, 'Soviet tanks on the streets of Paris would bring mutual understanding and lots of time to discuss things.' In his 1966 novel *Beautiful Twentysomethings*, Hłasko presents us with another variation on this theme: 'It is impossible to pass along experience. We can only convince the residents of Paris or Milan, who dream of communism, of its deficiency when Soviet tanks appear on their city streets.'

What has changed since then? Almost nothing. OK, the USSR did collapse, and the communist project has basically failed. But Russia, which 'united' that USSR, has remained pretty much the same as it's always been: a senseless gathering of stolen territories founded on a fundamental lie, saturated with unsubstantiated imperial ambitions. Unsubstantiated because other empires – classical empires, for example – subjugated native peoples but also attempted to raise them up to their own cultural/civilizational standards, at least a little. When Russia enslaved people who were more developed than they were, they simply buried them in the abyss of Russia's barbarism. And it has no intention of stopping doing so.

After all, continental Europe – by which I don't mean Poland or the Baltic countries, but the part that doesn't remember Soviet tanks on its city streets – remained the same, if not from time immemorial, then for quite a long time: a mannered prostitute who contorts herself into Joan of Arc. Truth be told, optimists say that Europe is beginning to see things a bit more clearly now. Personally, I'm not sure. When I look at the billions that Europe continues to pour into the Russian economy daily and the Russophilia printed by the French, Italian, Spanish and Portuguese press, my scepticism increases.*

Germany and Hungary are two pathological examples. Both Germany and Hungary should remember Russian tanks well, but alas they do not seem to. The German pathology has obvious psychological explanations that are completely foreign to Russians: a sense of guilt for the crimes of ancestors. It's unclear why the Germans use this sense so selectively, why they don't apply it to Ukrainians in whose lands their grandfathers and great-grandfathers carried out most of their atrocities. For the life of me I can't comprehend Hungary in general, and Orbán specifically.

But then again, if for the past month and a half the behaviour of certain people has been difficult to comprehend, then what can you say about Orbán, who is only externally akin to a person? He, not caring what anyone else thinks, and to the great joy of his spiritual brother in the Kremlin, supposes that the massacre in Bucha was waged by Ukraine. If I were

---

* This was the author's opinion at the time he wrote the essay.

authorized to do so, I, too, wouldn't care what anyone thought; perhaps I would theorize that Budapest-56 was staged by the Hungarians.*

Timothy Snyder, as if speaking particularly to Orbán and the other European political hacks from both the right and left, has clearly and simply condemned the genocidal character of the Russian regime, though it's a futile endeavour. The Russian regime is like the Third Reich: it condemns Ukrainians to death simply because they are not Russian. At the same time, Dmitry Medvedev, the most pathetic of Putin's patsies, has joined Orbán in stating that the Bucha and Mariupol genocides were faked, once again repeating that absurdity about the 'denazification and demilitarization of Ukraine', and openly (we should be thankful for that) declared that: 'in the name of peace for future generations of Ukrainians themselves', Russia plans to 'build an open Eurasia – from Lisbon to Vladivostok'.

Do the grandsons and great-grandsons of Nazis among EU politicians today hear Medvedev? Did European politicians, who still do not dare try everything they can to stop Putin and save not only us but themselves too, hear him? Do politicians not understand that when liberal, democratic Europe invested astronomical sums in Russia for decades, Russia used that money to develop parties and movements that aim to destroy that very liberal, democratic Europe and build a 'Ruzzian'† world from Vladivostok to Lisbon?

---

* During the 1956 Hungarian Revolution, when Hungarians protested against their government's domestic policies and Soviet control, several protesters were shot and killed by state authorities.
† 'Ruzzia' is a neologism created during this war that combines 'Russia' with the letter 'z' – the symbol Russia has chosen to put on their tanks, etc.

World history occasionally arrives at a so-called bifurcation point, determining the fate of entire continents. Today, the future of Europe is being determined in Ukraine. Those who want to leave the bifurcation point, preserving their dignity and hanging on to their own identity, must overcome the hypocrisy, fear and nihilism intrinsic to politics. Even if European nations and leaders don't understand this, or pretend not to. In either case, it means that they deserve to have their countries transformed into Putin's Eurasia – one which doesn't recognize others' borders and is sown with thousands of Buchas and Mariupols. All the way to Lisbon.

Translated by Mark Andryczyk

Fortune Telling by Literary Works

Taras Prokhasko

14 April 2022

Someone from Yalivets – I don't remember whether it was
Franz or Sebastian – said that, in order to carry on being himself during the war, he talked the same way he did before. But
it was difficult for him to say where the war wasn't going on,
where it was already going on, where the war was still going
on, and where the war was no longer going on. Our situation,
after all, is the same.

In order to remain yourself, a person who not only speaks
but also listens, that is, reads, you must have at least something
other than instructions, reports and orders to read, in any
period of history. To read something in the language that you
try not to betray, in order to remain yourself. To survive and
not break. So that you can go on to read many more good
books. Or at least the best paragraphs from many different
books. So that the touch of beauty can be as fragmentary as its
nature, which presents itself to thought and experience with
the utmost subtlety.

It is very good when you remember just one fragment, a
few details, a sentence or several phrases from a major book.
And it's just as good when only one book fits into an
emergency escape-bag or a soldier's backpack. Then this
book – in a week-long train journey or during a short stay in a

prison cell – receives a thorough multistoried labyrinth of reading, of which even Borges would be envious.

There are also books that you absolutely must pack, neglecting everything else that turns out not to be so vital (such as matches, tourniquets, blankets and old photographs) when leaving home. There are books you leave in the house, doomed to destruction. Then there are those that may manage to remain more or less undamaged, after all that happened to your home while you were away.

And there are houses, more or less destroyed, in which there were no bookcases, houses without even a single book.

I remember several books from my childhood that came from the First World War. Fairy tales by Oscar Wilde, algebra by Leonhard Euler. I imagine an unrealistic X-ray: the belongings of soldiers and refugees from all sides revealing a huge library in different languages. I imagine a memorial composed of volumes and folios that were orphaned in trenches, knapsacks, entrenchments, marshes, gardens and fields, in ditches along the roads.

If there is something pleasant in life now, it is memories and thoughts of books. About the library of Carpathian smugglers in Jerzy Stempowski's writing, about Rilke's volumes, about closely watched trains in Bohumil Hrabal's novel, about the journey over Chornohora* for several bundles of books by ancient authors, and about Stanisław Vincenz.

I read *One Hundred Years of Solitude* while I was in the army. A long autonomous trip, so-called combat duty. Spring, a cold armoured car, Gabriel García Márquez. There were some unknown and forgotten railway tracks in the woods. I was

---

* The tallest mountain range in the Carpathian Mountains, whose name means 'Black Mountain'.

lying on a folded camouflage net on a high armoured deck. The sky was blue, the sun was intense, and the grass emerging from under the snows was wet and cold. The days were getting longer and the nights shorter. Birds were returning from the south. Thousands of fat frogs were making love on the rails and sleepers, very close, almost between the lines that seemed green to irritated eyes. They climbed on top of each other, sniffed, croaked, grunted, moved their feet and hands, hugged. The real Márquez. Real beauty. Real literature. The meaning of which is that you can hone something perfect.

Because – as the poet used to say – I won't die from war going on in the world . . . *

Translated by Alla Perminova and Michael M. Naydan

---

* This is a reference to the 1985 Yaroslav Dovhan poem 'Ne vid toho ia pomru' ('It's not from this I'll die'), which became the lyrics of a well-known song by Viktor Morozov in 1986.

A Cold Spring

Iryna Tsilyk

15 April 2022

There is nothing romantic about our wartime get-togethers, my husband and me. I grew up on mainly black-and-white films featuring beautiful women and men broken by circumstances, whose brief twentieth-century rendezvous were full of despair, emotional strain and passionate tenderness. I agonized with the protagonists, though their problems seemed alien to me. But now everything is close by, now I am that black-and-white woman with sad eyes. It's funny how things turn out.

Occasionally I think about one of our get-togethers at the start of the war in 2014. My husband had been serving in the Ukrainian army for almost a year, spending long months in trenches on the front line. He'd transformed from an urban writer and intellectual into a strange, exhausted soldier with dry, listless eyes and weathered hands. We had been dreaming about a meeting for a long time and it finally took place in the neutral territory of Severodonetsk, on the front line. But something between us had broken, disappeared, died. He was a strange person, a stranger. It was a warm spring and everything around us teemed with life. The delicate flowers on the Donbas cherry and apricot trees swelled with nectar. My husband and I tried to remember how to have a conversation and how it used to be to have one another close by. In a noisy, untidy apartment we'd rented for two days the insoles of someone else's combat boots lay on the radiator. I wept quietly in the bathroom, biting a towel, then washed with cold water and entered the room with a crooked smile. I thought, somehow things will work out.

Later, that is what happened. My husband was discharged and returned home. It took him about six months to get used to living a peaceful life again. Years have passed since then and I recently learned a startling and uncomfortable truth, that when he returned from the front he had had suicidal thoughts. I had not noticed anything at all. I only saw a lost and lonely Kai with an icicle in his heart. Time passed, I cried and cried, and my husband's heart thawed. He became warm, familiar and alive once again.

Did I ever think that we'd have to go through this experience again? I couldn't help but wonder whether we would. Why live in denial? We are a generation with emergency escape-bags on our back. We lived like that for eight years. But nevertheless we decided that it was time to build homes, raise kids, and be happy together. Somehow things will work out.

In the last months before the full-scale invasion, we sensed that all this tenderness, peacefulness, cosiness, the everyday plans, the carefully selected books and art, the tickets purchased in springtime for distant journeys, were all hanging by a thread. We lived the whole winter like this, swinging around emotionally: we would gather emergency escape-bags and then make fun of ourselves; we believed the American intelligence and awaited the Big War but then spontaneously bought tickets to celebrate New Year's Eve in Paris. We talked and stayed silent, laughed then cried. Once I was drinking wine at our place with two girlfriends, both war veterans. 'Right now, I'm healing my back,' one of them shared offhandedly. 'I always wonder whether I'll dare to have a baby, finally, or whether I'll have to put a bulletproof vest on once again.' We were all thinking the same thing.

The night of 23–24 February was the first good night's sleep I'd had in days. But I was woken at 7 a.m. by my husband's hushed voice: 'Irka! They're bombing Kyiv! They're bombing cities!' I began to run. In my own apartment, in circles. I scrolled the news, listened to the sirens in astonishment, and gathered important documents while stubbornly cooking some soup; I wasn't planning on going anywhere yet. I listened to every sound and feigned calmness in front of our eleven-year-old son. While running from room to room I stumbled upon the packed gloomy green heap of my husband's bag. On top of it lay his filled-out army documents. And then, right in that moment, my heart cracked, and life once again broke into *before* and *after*.

We have gone through so much in the days of this new open war. My chest is now burned-out, hollow. I just can't get warm. On the forty-sixth day I saw my husband for the first time. Before then we'd had weeks of calls, and messages every morning and evening. My son celebrated his birthday in Lviv without his father. 'Unfortunately, the war has hindered me from being with you on your birthday for a second time,' his father wrote to him. Déjà vu, I thought, and I couldn't rid myself of that feeling when I made the trip to see my husband.

This time we didn't meet in Severodonetsk but in our dear Kyiv. In Severodonetsk, by the way, most of the houses and apartments have been destroyed by the Russians. I wonder whether that apartment in Severodonetsk remembers the awkward tenderness of the soldier exhausted by life and his wife with the shattered heart, and whether it is still alive. Either way, we now had the opportunity to meet in our own apartment, which we bought a year ago, having dreamed of our own place for fifteen years. For a whole year we wove the nest we'd dreamed of. Now, I wonder what the point of it all was. Renovations and libraries? Why do we need pillows that match our furniture? Why was I buying a fancy porcelain teapot two weeks before the war? So that someone can ruin our world with one ballistic missile? But our apartment is still intact, and thank God for that.

I arrived in Kyiv from Lviv late in the evening. My train was very late and the curfew had begun and, while I was still in the train carriage, I heard that I wouldn't be able to leave the station until morning. Ahead of us was our planned night, the only night of freedom my husband had. I hadn't expected this. Swallowing my tears, I counted the minutes, surrounded by the clatter of train wheels, and attempted to read Hemingway's short stories. It was the first time in a month and a half that I had picked up a book. The distant world of the 1920s seemed uninteresting, unimportant, unexpectedly empty. Only one story, 'Soldier's Home', caused my stomach to flutter.

I didn't end up spending the night at the train station. My husband suddenly appeared, so familiar, so different, in his army uniform. He silently pulled me towards him and confidently led me outside, past the train station security; no one said anything. His commander's car was waiting outside and we rushed off into the night, into the empty Kyiv streets, stopping only once to give a password at the checkpoint. Tired, hungry, having not bought any food or, moreover, wine (stores don't open late under martial law), we went home. It was so cold there; the heating had been shut off earlier than usual. In our son's room the radiator had leaked and now the wooden floor swelled and buckled, completely altering the familiar surface. And it seemed we had our neighbour's cockroaches: hordes of dead and living insects were scattered over my refined apartment, my white kitchen.

It wasn't like it was in the films. I would prefer to have seen myself in a little black dress and black seamed tights, eyes dark from arousal and a voice cracked with passion. Like the heroine in the Pawlikowski film *Cold War* who is both terribly happy and unhappy. Fractured fates, the unbearable lightness of being, *dwa serduszka cztery oczy oj o joj.** All the ingredients were there, except for the fact that I had unbrushed hair, was wearing two sweaters and looking sadly at socks that had *Ukrainian Armed Forces* written on them, hanging to dry on our beautiful wooden stools, bought a year ago to host our friends.

Messy, tired, cold. This is how these brief meetings and long farewells take place. Emotional stupor is an important guarantee of life in war because, having allowed yourself to feel anything at all, you are now at great risk of collapsing into bottomless agony. The sadness of our youth, which is being stolen from us by the enemy. Our plans for the future. The impossibility of building homes, giving birth to children, of being carefree. There lie Kai and Gerda, silent and unable to get warm. Who will melt the ice in their hearts?

The next day we left our apartment and headed in different directions: me to take care of our son and to battle on the

---

* A line from the theme song 'Dwa Serduszka Cztery Oczy' for the 2019 Paweł Pawlikowski film *Cold War*. The line translates into English as 'Two hearts, four eyes, oh no'.

cultural front, my husband to investigate the results of the bloody atrocities conducted by the Russians in the Kyiv region. Time and again I monitor the long-term weather forecast. It's supposed to get warmer soon, much warmer. It must, right?

Translated by Mark Andryczyk

Three Springs, Two Lives, One War

Volodymyr Rafeyenko

28 April 2022

Everything has an end and a beginning. How things turn out depends on where you mark the starting point. For most people who follow the news from the front, Russia's war with Ukraine began on 24 February 2022. But, as for many other Ukrainians, it entered my family's and my life in the spring of 2014.

A very peculiar spring arrived in Donetsk in 2014. Before the war I, young and handsome, would run every morning in the park. I remember being astonished by the natural world then. Heavy rains fell. Thunderstorms began earlier than usual. In the evening and in the afternoon, in the morning and at night, the sky was a fiery yellow and red and the landscape was thundering and stirring. Lightning struck, joyful and terrifying. Rain fell as if a heavenly curtain had opened over the city and blue-green water poured from above, as if washing us off the face of the earth. Then an incredible amount of ants, insects, mice and snails suddenly appeared smack dab in the centre of the city, where we lived. They swarmed, ran, walked, sat and swam. It seemed like the green rains would sweep all the human world away and that our European culture would be replaced with the culture of half-intelligent insects, fleas and all kinds of other muck (in the end that is what happened, but we only came to understand this later). Trees and plants grew bizarrely tall. The bushes by the entrance of our building grew half a metre in just a few days.

At night I dreamed melancholy, post-apocalyptic dreams. I was trying to survive during a nuclear conflict. In the morning I would shrug my shoulders, slowly dress, and go for a run in the half-dark city park for the sake of my mental and physical health. I had to keep to a routine; a person needs that in order to keep going, regardless of the state of things, right up until the very end.

Our park was enormous and, even though it was located at the very centre of an industrial city with a population of one million, had pheasants. Adults smiled at them and kids would chase them sometimes, without much success. Those birds didn't realize how lucky they were. They were cared for diligently and were a point of pride for everyone who lived in the city. There were other species of birds there, too, endless varieties. No one offended them. Everyone fed and watched over them with tenderness.

But in spring 2014 the birds' behaviour began to elicit some serious questions, at least for me. They started acting very strangely, though they weren't aggressive. They shrieked at me, escorted me along the paths I jogged on, jumped at my chest, landed on my shoulders and basically did not let me pass. One afternoon my wife and I were strolling through the park and decided to sit on a bench. It was getting warmer, we wanted to relax and warm our faces in the sun. Within just a few minutes a group of birds had assembled beside us and a small bird, a starling I believe, landed right on my knee and began screaming at me. I looked at my wife, she looked at me, and we smiled feebly. Conflicting feelings came over me.

Nature was obviously trying to tell us something. But at the time it was unclear what it was trying to say. After some time, I realized: it was chasing us from our home, trying to save us through these birds. The starling was yelling: 'Volodia, Olesia, run away from here! Barbarians are coming, and life will become completely impossible here!' On the other hand, the Universe was, in a way, using this flourishing to counter the death that was to take over this city, this region and our blessed steppe within half a year. Hundreds and thousands of deaths would take place here, according to the will of Russians, who would arrive under the banner of protecting Russian-speaking inhabitants. The tragic irony of all of this is that my entire family and I are Russian speakers. At least we were until 2014. But we did not need protection from anyone, not from our fatherland and not from the Ukrainian language, the first language of both my grandmothers.

Spring 2022 was just as strange and insane. By then my wife and I had been living near Kyiv for eight years; we'd had to leave Donetsk in June 2014. The cottage community where we had lived for the past six years was between Bucha and Borodianka, cities now known to everyone. But our community isn't on any map and probably never will be. Instead that territory made up of a string of cottage homes is designated as Blyzhni Sady (Nearby Orchards). Those orchards stretched out along Lake Gloria, huge, clean and deep. Blyzhni Sady's location, between the lake and a pine-tree forest, had always been the object of our silent and silly pride. Why not? We're just homeless refugees, but what we have here is like a holiday resort.

The house we lived in belonged to our friends, who were letting us live there. But within a few years it had become our home, too. All our other homes, including our native city, had become occupied territories through a process that was never outright called a military conflict. Just as the trees, rains and birds had warned us, Russian soldiers entered our city, and we had to abandon everything and move to Kyiv. And then we ended up at this resort.

Then, suddenly, we couldn't believe it: that very same 2014 Donetsk spring arrived in this resort in 2021. Startling early thunderstorms and copious rains. There was a sharp, abnormal growth of all kinds of plants. And finally, one quiet, warm day, birds fell upon us from the heavens. We were stunned, pleased, to see so many different birds. Listen, although we had lived in between Gloria and the pine forest for a while, we'd never seen anything like this. People who'd lived there for a long time couldn't remember a calamity like this ever happening before. Loads of large birds flew in, species never before seen here – about three dozen swans, for example. White storks danced in the sky as if they had lost their minds. The smaller birds (we didn't count how many) would fly from one place to another in clouds. It was a true spring of birds.

I was going through a difficult illness at the time, so my wife and I would walk by the lake daily regardless of the weather. I needed to recuperate and strolling in the woods after a long and cold winter was psychologically difficult for people from the steppe like us. We sought the sky, space and clouds. We needed air and wind. It blew above the dam that separated Gloria and the valley of the Zdvyzh river, the strengthening, healing wind.

I followed spring from its beginning to its end while strolling, and I couldn't help but see parallels. I wouldn't let myself voice the thoughts that entered my head, even to myself. *'There's been a spring like this before,'* I thought, as I looked at the tall, strikingly blue, pristine sky above me, *'and similar birds too. There are even more birds this spring than in 2014, the rains more copious, and lightning is striking like never before. Exactly half a year after that spring, it began slowly, and after a year it flared up and then kept going. I wonder whether the same thing will happen here, exactly one year later.'* I was afraid of saying this to my wife. But she saw everything, too, and was thinking the same thing. She wouldn't look at me when I told her funny stories, or sang, or recited some poems, when I tried to cheer up my Olesia, to try to lift my own worries.

In the first half of February 2022 it suddenly became warmer and, after 10 February, a potent and early spring arrived. But the warmer and more pleasant that things were outside, the more frightening the international news and the prognoses of experts became. My wife and I heard all of it, we read the news, but nevertheless tried to believe that this cup would pass from us. We felt we were living double lives.

In one of our lives, a cruel, profane, hopelessly horrific life, there was the daily news, military analysis about a Russian attack on Ukraine, predictions, maps of potential movements of Russian armies, and phone calls to friends where we discussed it all endlessly. Predictions slammed into our hearts like birds, circled, screamed, disrupted our thoughts, and ushered in feelings of blackness, of being trapped with no way out.

In the other life we were preparing, simultaneously, for two happy events.

The first, a major one: my trip to the United States, long planned by my friends and publishers. In March, Harvard University Press was supposed to publish an English-language translation of my novel *Mondegreen: Songs about Death and Love*. Presentations, appearances, readings and lectures had already been arranged. I was supposed to be in the US from the middle of April until the middle of May all in all. A few days before the fully fledged war began I paid my registration fee and waited for an invitation to my visa interview. As it turned out, the US embassy had already closed down, and now it looked like I'd have to go to Warsaw for a visa. But I was ready to do anything to go on this trip.

The second was a private, quiet family event. My wife and I were preparing for our wedding anniversary, which falls on 24 February, the day that my Olesia once said her definitive 'yes', and we officially became husband and wife.

We tried to keep our two lives, the light and the dark, apart with all our energy. We didn't want them to know anything about one another. On 23 February we discussed what to eat for our anniversary meal. We were up on the second floor, in a room where the windows face west, where the sun takes so long to set that you can write a poem before it has finished setting. I thought about what we would do that evening. The past days had been busy and I was exhausted. The night between 23 and 24 February, for perhaps the first time in a while, I fell into a deep sleep.

On 24 February a fully fledged war began. And within just a few days Blyzhni Sady, our nearby orchards, were surrounded by the Russian army in a tight circle.

Translated by Mark Andryczyk

To You, Beloved River

Taras Prokhasko

28 April 2022

I was in the Vinnytsia region sometime in the middle of January. It seems strange, but now it is almost impossible to remember exactly what happened in mid-January. But those bizarre pre-war months were taking place then – a kind of chronicle of announced death which, with its saturation of all kinds of messages, surpassed the reports from the still-living COVID-19 front. Try to remember, all our cities were terror-stricken with fake mines. Schools were evacuated in Vinnytsia. But we went further than that. Through deciduous forests, to the tributaries of the Buh River.

From a tall bank I could see wide valleys, basins and lowlands, bends, ravines, overgrown oaks which converged like ribs to the ridge of the great river. In quiet ecstasy I realized that this is Ukraine. I was born in another area, grew up in another space, lived my life in a completely different landscape. But in all the pictures I have seen, ever since childhood, all the songs, all the borrowed myths into which we fixed ourselves, all the sounds and colours – here they are. In a few minutes my knowledge of the Galician – Carpathian landscape was gushing with a certain deceitfulness in the framework of this landscape. It was as if I'd visited the distant backdrop of vivid, ancient images.

Then it started to snow and the wind began to blow. We walked through the hills, sometimes hiding behind them from the storm, but more often crawling into it. I thought about the Galicians from the Ukrainian Galician Army* who fought and died here. I thought that they must have felt something similar. That it was all worth fighting for. It's a pity to die, but there's no better place for it.

When people sometimes say that this is our land, it's mostly not about resources and territories. Landscape comprises something seen by the brain of the heart and the heart of the brain. It is something faithful and infallible. To be able to be yourself in your landscape is to be in harmony with your inner and outer world.

When I visit Lemkivshchyna,† I see my homeland laid bare, thanks to the lines and shading of the image of the land.

Once I was travelling by train from Uzhhorod (in Western Ukraine) to Moscow. I focused my attention on how the homesteads and territories had been arranged and how they had evolved. The colourful flower gardens of Transcarpathia, the exquisite, lush order of Galicia, the green-coloured flourishing of Greater Ukraine, the elaborate designers' layout near Kyiv, the modest charm of neat Slobozhanshchyna,‡ traces of ethnic borders in the Bryansk region, the lapidary nature and monumentality of decay of the Moscow region. There were only grey houses behind board fences, bare yards without

---

* The armed forces of the Western Ukrainian Peoples' Republic that were active until November 1919.
† The region where the Ukrainian ethnic group the Lemkos live, which is currently located along the Polish – Slovak border and the Carpathian Mountains.
‡ The Sloboda region of north east Ukraine and south west Russia.

flowers and trees, only an outhouse and a pile of garbage in the corner.

As a biologist I have always shared Dudayev's* evaluation of Russian proclivities. He aptly stated that Russian devastation concerns not only people and culture, nor manifestations of civilization, but nature, too. I can only imagine how it felt for the Chechens, whose life was lived in such a rich but vulnerable mountainous landscape.

Scorched earth, which has always been the lodestar of Russian strategy, implies, among other things, the total destruction of landscapes, which are a defining feature of patriotism and are the foundation of identity for populations that have been destroyed. Having ruined the landscape, it is very easy to knock the ground from under anyone's feet. Because what is the value of a creature deprived of its distinctive ecotope?

In the end, we all know our own value. Let flowers, cucumbers, apricots, cherries and chestnuts be . . . the worst thing is that we ourselves used to destroy our landscapes every day. And there aren't fewer hidden rubbish dumps than there are ones in full view. But the time has come. Cleaning up after the destroyers, we can clean up after our former selves without pomp. Without making it too clear that it was we who did this. And clearly knowing that next time it would be unkind to blame the invaders for the entire mess.

Translated by Alla Perminova and Michael M. Naydan

---

* The Chechen separatist leader Dzhokhar Dudayev (1944–1996), who was assassinated by a Russian missile strike.

From Zinc to Polyethylene

Andriy Bondar

16 May 2022

It so happens that the backdrop of Russia's war against Ukraine makes us see Afghanistan in two different ways at once. On the one hand it is a Central Asian country, remote enough not to evoke intense emotions in the context of our current dramatic experiences in Ukraine. On the other hand, it is close enough and significant enough for us not to be able to neglect it.

Afghanistan is a symbol both of several defeats and of the inability of any foreign force to cope with a contradictory and understudied cultural, political and tribal entity.

The history of the last forty-something years has shown that the powers-that-be have learned little from breaking their teeth on this incomprehensible country. Afghanistan withstood almost a decade-long invasion of the so-called 'limited contingent of Soviet forces' (1979–89), the end of which, in fact, crowned the collapse of the 'greatest geopolitical catastrophe' of all time – the Soviet Union. Last year Afghanistan saw a great renaissance of the Taliban, the most conservative Islamist movement, which finally showed the Western world the futility of attempts to artificially launch modernization into a feudal society characterized by almost total religious obscurantism.

Afghanistan proves the enduring truth of old principles: it is impossible to defeat and conquer an enemy you do not know, do not understand and, most importantly, do not feel; it is impossible to defeat an enemy if you do not fully understand why you need to defeat it and what you will do with it after the victory; and, finally, it is impossible to impose on the conquered country values that it does not share either *en masse* or at the level of its political elites – if, of course, it is appropriate to apply such a risky term as 'elite' to the Taliban leaders (which I personally doubt). And not because I have become a captive of another orientalism but, on the contrary, because Afghanistan itself has proven by its very existence the inability and historical weakness of any orientalist approaches on the grand chessboard.

The point here is not in the fundamental cultural and political 'superiority' of some and, accordingly, 'underdevelopment' of others, but rather in the fact that this superiority mistakenly attributes to itself the ability to freely edit the incomprehensible in its own way and to organize it according to its own rules and principles.

The 'superiority' of Soviet culture over the mujahideen in the eighties was based on socialism. It presumed the existence of a universal method of building the state and society, capable of levelling the contradictions inherent in history and culture, and abolishing all biases, forming the foundations of the inexorable progress of the Soviet model with the inevitable celebration of the triumph of the most progressive system. The 'superiority' of Western (mostly American) culture over the Taliban rested in democracy. It assumed that if a 'prejudiced' society was exposed to the democratic procedures of freedom of expression, to painted bright signs on newly created institutions, and was provided with modern weapons, it would certainly overcome the darkness in itself and around it, and therefore would reveal to the world another miracle of the victory of democracy and freedom over autocracy and the enslavement of the individual.

None of these imaginary 'superiorities' has changed the main issue: even clearly demonstrating the civilizational, cultural, institutional and technological beauties of its model, it is impossible to invent the traditions of democracy and to eliminate contradictions formed over the centuries, so therefore it is impossible to do what is inherent in every foreign invasion – to transplant its idea of the meaning of existence and human happiness onto a foreign sandy soil.

Afghanistan might be called the most unhappy country in the world if we knew for sure that the Afghan idea of happiness and unhappiness coincides with ours. It would also be tempting to talk about this country as a victim of geopolitical circumstances, if we knew for sure that someone in Afghanistan thinks in terms of geopolitics or calculates any political strategies in advance. We could rightly say that a country deprived of its subjectivity is doomed to suffer, if we knew exactly how Afghans imagine their own eventual subjectivity, and in what context they regard their recent suffering.

Afghanistan is *terra incognita*, in contact with which empires collapse and geopolitical doctrines fail. By its very existence this country has saved the countries of our region at least twice in the last forty years. If Brezhnev had not sent Soviet troops to Afghanistan in 1979, he might have been smart and talented enough to send them to Poland in 1981, as he did to Czechoslovakia some thirteen years before. And it is unknown how the Berlin Wall would have fallen then, and how the countries of the Eastern bloc would have been freed from communism. If last year President Biden had not suffered a stunning defeat in Afghanistan he would not be as reckless and passionate about helping Ukraine now. Only a lazy man has not made this observation in Ukraine.

Therefore, in a sense, the vicissitudes of this country in collision with the outside world often give opportunities to other nations. Fifteen thousand dead Soviet soldiers in distant Afghanistan over more than nine years, leading to the collapse of the Soviet Union, and almost twice this number of dead Russian soldiers in Ukraine in less than three months: this all testifies to the fact that Russia at the beginning of the third decade of the twenty-first century is in a much worse state of consciousness than the USSR was in its twilight, ruled by a geriatric leadership that in 1985 decided to save the system by electing a Gorbachev, a younger man.

Therefore, Afghanistan is for us also a unit of measurement of the temperature of the empire, which for the last eighty-two days of the war has actually suffered two defeats in the Afghan war in terms of numbers of lives lost but has not yet fully realized how advanced and incurable the diseases of 'flight from freedom' and 'death wish' are. Because, I repeat, it is impossible to defeat an enemy you do not know, do not understand and, most importantly, do not feel. It is impossible to simply declare your own imperial identity as your primary value and not cease to exist after that.

I will remember for the rest of my life a fragment of an interview with a Soviet officer, I think, that appeared in the newspaper *Komsomolskaya Pravda* (*The Truth of the Komsomol*) in the late 1980s, when the winds of change were already blowing in full force. Somewhere on his combat mission the officer spotted a lizard on a large stone, which froze stock-still, with its head turned to the right, utterly demonstrating complete indifference to everything that was happening there and then – to the explosions, screams, fire and destruction. The lizard just kept sitting on the stone. And to the surprise of this officer, a month later he found the very same lizard in the very same position on the very same stone. That's how incomprehensible it was, this Afghanistan, this distant, scorching East. Why did we come to this motionless and terrible horror? You could read between the lines. Although a much more serious and substantial question for this and all subsequent Russian officers is: where and in what condition will you all return after this? Afghanistan gave its answer to the Russian soldier. Ukraine will do the same. Another thing is that he, as always, will not hear or understand anything. A zinc coffin does not transmit sound very well. Not to mention the polyethylene (of body bags).

Translated by Alla Perminova and Michael M. Naydan

Planning the Past

Volodymyr Rafeyenko

5 May 2022

Everything that has begun will continue, ceaselessly and relentlessly. I had this thought on the evening of the second day of the war. The war, which we had expected but was somehow so sudden, had already cruelly and firmly taken over our entire lives. We ended up in a different new reality against our will, one where everything was terrifying, perhaps because it was impossible to believe it was real.

By the afternoon of 24 February there was continual fighting between our home and Kyiv. The simple knowledge of that fact elicited terror. Our minds refused to come to grips with reality. How is it possible that between us and the capital – a distance, for goodness sake, of no more than thirty kilometres – Russian armies, tanks, armoured personnel carriers and heavy artillery were now found. This was unfathomable; it couldn't possibly be true.

But it was precisely that which we could not fathom that kept us from sleeping, living and breathing. On the roads that led to Kyiv, right next to us, Armageddon was happening. The house was shaking and ringing like a frightened old bell from all the shooting, both in the daytime and at night. To the right of us and to the left, and above us too. Planes and helicopters flew at Kyiv and at Hostomel. In the evening and at night a

73

flash blazed above the lake. We couldn't believe what we were seeing.

We only had sporadic phone reception and it wasn't always possible to reach everyone, but the internet worked surprisingly well. We followed the news non-stop, twenty-four hours a day. Something implausible was taking place all over the country. The Russians were launching rockets at large cities and waging an attack from many sides simultaneously. And, by the looks of things, they were rather successful. They sliced through to the capital like a knife through butter. It was unimaginable.

All of this, and the constant pounding – our home shook and air itself rolled in waves – was incomprehensible for our cat Parmesan. He refused to go outside and tried to hide, but where can you hide from constant explosions when your building doesn't have a basement? Honestly, I was in such shock that I would have also preferred to hide somewhere and sleep until the end of the war. Until the end of Russia. To the bitch's end. Until that country is replaced with a large black ocean, frigid like the Cosmos. I imagined that might be possible: you would lie down in a bed that was shuttered from explosions and unexpectedly fall asleep. You awake and Russia no longer exists. None of its tanks, artillery, no Putin or Dostoyevsky, no Lavrov or Tolstoy, none of those 'brothers', no nation crippled by its own 'great culture'. There would be nothing there now except an ocean. Like Malevich's 'Black Square', it would be an abyss. A little seagull would sing, sounding like 'Ode to Joy'.

Despite the shock we needed to do something or we would lose our minds. We were preparing emergency escape-bags and calamity suitcases, packing away things we needed, counting money, gathering official documents and then misplacing them, searching for them for hours, finding them, and trying to make transportation arrangements, so that my Olesia, at least, could be taken away from this beautiful resort. We did all this carefully and sincerely. But we now had nowhere to go. Literally. All the roads surrounding us had been transformed into a theatre of war. None of the local drivers were willing to take the risk. They suggested that we wait, at least for a few days. Travelling the Warsaw Road was lethally dangerous, they said. The entire road, at least the part near us, where the exits for the cooperatives, homesteads and villages are, was stacked with Russian military equipment. The situation on the Zhytomyr Road was even more precarious: there were intense battles taking place there. Based on the nonstop pounding, and according to rumour, our forces were attacking the Russian equipment day and night. Where are you planning to go', they said. Who's waiting for you there? Moreover, the latest driver we were trying to get to take us away pointed out, they say there are small groups of motorized Russian troops heading towards Kyiv from the Belarusian border constantly. No one could predict when and where they might suddenly appear on the road.

The fuel problems were obvious. Those who had fuel didn't want to waste it on us, as they didn't know whether they would be able to find any petrol stations on the way back. So on the evening of the second day we realized we should relax a bit. No one was going anywhere any more. There was nothing to go to, nowhere to go, not even a reason to go. Who said where we were going would be any safer? If the Russians had already brought their wonderful culture all the way here, near Kyiv, so that we could benefit from its marvellous treasures, then perhaps in a few days they'd bring it to Lviv, too. Or to Ivano-Frankivsk, or Transcarpathia.

The explosions were terrifying. They made the ground shake. In these two months many Ukrainians have suffered the horror of 'the arrival', of sudden roaring black death. But you know what? In my experience, it only really gets difficult after the second or third day, when the explosions haven't stopped for even an hour. There's nowhere to run. You're pinched between a forest, between pine trees, pleasantly and warmly yellow in the glow of the February sun, and a lake, beautiful, deep and clean like death itself. You feel trapped here for ever and ever, just an ordinary guy who wants to live and breathe day and night. But there's no guarantee you'll live even an hour longer. In the horror that consumes you there is something inhuman which you must battle to preserve, at least a fraction of dignity. You can't be afraid all the time and you can't depend on the cruel, merciless acts of a culture, even one as beautiful as Russian culture. You need to do something to hang on to at least a little self-respect. To be able to smile when you look into your wife's dark, tired eyes. It is more difficult for her, she depends on you. There is no one else in the world who can help her get through the chasm of these days of death and helplessness.

The end of February was very warm. I went outside early one day to stretch my legs, get some fresh air, and maybe do some chores. There were things one could do to avoid sitting in that building we'd been trapped in for three days in a row now, swinging over an abyss of nonexistence, feeling the rhythms pulsate through the walls and the explosions and reverberations that arrived through the forest. Swallowing my first gulp of fresh air, I began to pray. No matter what, I would talk to the Lord and the Virgin Mary. I asked him how they were up there in Heaven. Whether everything was OK. If there weren't too many souls arriving there over the past couple of days. I told them how the night had passed. They were interested in my opinions on contemporary Russian literature and cinema, and I told them that I haven't read or watched that crap for eight years now. That if it was up to me I would go back to the eighties and after I finished high school I would apply to go to any university that was located in western Ukraine. Lviv Ivan Franko National University or Chernivtsi Yuri Fedkovych National University, to Lviv Polytechnical University or even to the Danylo Halytsky Medical University. I'm not much of a medic, I said to Maria, but at least I would have learned the Ukrainian language much earlier. I would have become a surgeon, travelled to Moscow, gone down to its deepest Metro station and cut the heart out of that cursed city.

You could say that I was planning the past. I don't think I can explain this in a short essay or even a book of essays. So I'm writing a novel with that exact title: *Planning the Past in Wartime Conditions*. Only fiction is capable of communicating the reality of those days: the sorrow, the hope, the weather. The weather was very strange. From the second week of February until nearly the end of the month it was incredibly warm and sunny. It felt like a sudden summer would kick in any day. The explosions and constant smoke made me worry about forest fires, which were entirely possible in conditions like that. We lived almost in the forest itself. Any forest fire could bring our end. I didn't want an early summer. I asked God to hold it back or, at least, not let it come too early. OK, whatever you say, was the answer.

And then at the end of the month winter began to get the upper hand. The sun went into hiding. Grey twilights arrived, which made explosions sound metaphysical. Life had lost its sense, its direction and its storyline, too. We didn't understand how or where to live. What kind of story will flow from what we managed to sense in the first days of the war? Are we really still alive or are we just dreaming about one another? And then, in a few days, the morning temperature stuck at -15°C and we started to lose our electricity, mobile phone reception, water and internet.

Translated by Mark Andryczyk

Complete Dissolution

Andriy Bondar

31 May 2022

In the 2017 documentary series *The Putin Interviews* by the Kremlin's useful idiot Oliver Stone, there is a telling moment where Vladimir Putin talks about his grandfather Spiridon's experiences in the First World War. During a battle his grandfather shot an Austrian soldier with his Shantz gun, and then immediately ran with a first-aid kit to bandage the wounded man and try to save his life. 'If he had not shot him, the Austrians would have killed him,' Putin explained to Stone.

This episode reflects the essence of the Russian president's moral image: thanks to the unverified past of a practically unknown person, Putin attempts to justify his 'pre-emptive' decision in 2014 when he annexed Crimea and occupied Donbas. That's a superficial conclusion, calculated to appeal to the Russian audience or Putin's uncritical followers in the West who are susceptible to cheap techniques.

Russian propaganda is just axe-grinding. Besides literally overlaying current patterns of behaviour on the distant past, which propagates Russia's historical myth that it always has to defend itself (Putin does not explain to Stone what Russia actually did in that war in sending Putin's grandfather there), and the 'eternal' character of Putinism as a sanctified, legitimate methodology of political behaviour (Putinism appeared before Putin was even born, sprouting from historical Russia, which supposedly only waged just wars), there is also a personal, mental level to this microplot. The loyal viewer is offered a fear neither shown nor uttered. Putin's grandfather *had to* defend himself to avoid the worst-case scenario – death – which also insinuates the possibility of Vladimir Vladimirovich never having being born, a real phobia and catastrophe for any narcissistic psychopath; second only to the collapse of the USSR, of course.

For the past three months I have been visiting the website of Russia's Radio Liberty, along with the documentary TV channel Current Time in Prague, which sometimes shows videos where Russian passers-by are interviewed about the course of the so-called 'special military operation' and its consequences for the country and for themselves. There is something striking and disturbing in their voices, which at first I could not understand. The most interesting thing is not that 80 per cent of them strongly support their president and his policy, but that when they are stopped while walking they discard their private essence within seconds and assume the guise of a person owned by the state, devoid of personal features. They seem to put on the invisible uniform of a 'servant' and deny their own individuality. They do not pretend to be Putin and do not copy him, but for a few seconds they become him, erasing themselves instantly.

It's not that they are just trying to obediently re-transmit the Kremlin's propaganda and repeat Putin's doctrine on the TV shows of Vladimir Solovyov and Olga Skabeyeva. They are not just demonstrating their verbal loyalty and understanding of politics, they are also manifesting themselves as reproductive organs of his supreme will through their facial expressions, gestures and even their tone of voice. Every other interviewee immediately adopts Putin's way of formulating sentences and copies his logic.

This is not just a reproduction of Putin's picture of the world but a complete masochistic dissolution in him, he who has been dictating his will for twenty-two years, transferring his phobias, characteristics and contortions to them – those Dostoyevsky-style irrational head-scratchings that provide a spiritual connection to the Russian world where everyone is always on duty. It doesn't matter how old they are, eighteen or sixty-five, nor what their social status is or which cities they live in. And it doesn't matter whether they are really unconditionally devoted to his political doctrine and ready to fulfil it to the end. It doesn't even matter whether they fully understand everything they're saying.

The important thing is that this is a sign of collective dissolution in the image of the leader, an unconscious desire to copy not only his words but also what lies behind them. It is important to believe, to belong to a monolithic discourse that gives you conviction in your own truth and tells you that this truth is total and unconditional, that it has always been in you. Just as there has always been an 'eternal Putin', continuing his military-imperial subjugation and violence. They are accustomed to violence, they tolerate it, they recognize it as the core of their existence and their main export.

When they talk in the West today about 'one man's war', they once again offer us a riddle about the chicken and the egg, and also attempt, simply and beautifully, to separate the leader from his people. Western counter-propaganda hints at the 'alien nature' of Putin and his regime, attacking this fascist love for the father of the nation in the hope of seeing cracks in the monolith. But these attempts are illusory and naive. They'll never want to kill the father and be orphaned. None of them wishes that Putin had never been born. Everyone loves and cherishes his actions and words. Everyone shares responsibility for the blood and tears, destroyed cities, raped women and murdered children. Everyone wants him to live for ever, because they are nothing without violence. Without the sanction to commit violence, they are nothing. This is the only thing they have and what makes them one people.

A Russian mother who is given the star of a Russian hero for her paratrooper son killed in Ukraine finds it difficult to hold back tears. She eventually starts to cry. Because she is, after all, a mother. No Putin can destroy that. And so, crying – supposedly a frank human emotion that belongs to you only – turns into a symbol of faith. 'I am proud of our Vladimir Vladimirovich,' the mother says through tears, in Putin's voice and with Putin's aplomb of rightness and faith. She was not asked about that. She knows what to say and when and how to say it. They will all go with him to the very end. We need to remember this.

Translated by Alla Perminova and Michael M. Naydan

Blyzhni Sady (Nearby Orchards)

Volodymyr Rafeyenko

2 June 2022

No situation in life is so complex that it can't be made significantly worse. That particular truth doesn't hang around very long and is usually only realized, in all its beauty, when life displays its changeableness and incomprehensibility right before your eyes. We thought things were bad for us in the first days of the war: there was non-stop pounding, our building had no basement, and it was impossible to go anywhere. The blessed Russian culture had made it all the way up to Irpin and Bucha and attempted to seize Kyiv; it had poured down from the skies right onto the big Ukrainian cities and destroyed not only the young and the old but reality itself. We thought this was difficult, that it was difficult for us, that we found ourselves in a difficult situation and that we were at least brave, because we were holding on. Of course, we couldn't sleep or eat, we constantly watched the news and felt the horror growing inside us with the realization that we were closed off, both in time and space. We ended up inside a circle, surrounded by Russian occupational forces in the woods, but we kept up with events and updates from the headquarters of the Armed Forces of Ukraine and the Ministry of Foreign Affairs, we followed Zelensky, thanked Kuleba, prayed for Zaluzhny, listened to and watched Karpiak, attempted to converse in normal voices, and smiled diligently at one another.

'*But you're a tough guy,*' I said to myself somewhere in the depths of my heart, to encourage myself to continue living the incredibly eventful life that had been fated to me. '*You're strong, you're brave, just don't flinch, for Christ's sake, every time something explodes nearby, don't grab the edge of the couch. And exhale at least now and then because you've done nothing but inhale for the past three minutes, the lack of oxygen could kill you.*' What can you say, I mused, even my conversations with God have a measured character. All of this also contains an irresistible, bitter, pleasant wave of growing insanity, but no one can see that, no one except God, who's seen that and then some.

We've lost electricity, mobile reception and internet here. Honestly, I don't remember whether we still had internet when the building's water pump stopped working, or whether there was electricity, or whether we still had a mobile connection. But after about five or six hours everything shut down and we ended up in complete darkness. I turned my phone off, to preserve the battery, and examined my charger. At least the phone and charger were still OK. They'd been given to me by my colleagues and students before the war, because even then we would often lose our electricity and I'd have to present Zoom lessons using my phone as a WiFi hotspot. I thought of my colleagues, friends and students with gratitude, but wondered whether the charger would last much longer. What then? We'll think of something, but what if we don't have any electricity at all until the war ends? Where will we get water? We'd always had enough stored for a couple of days, a week maximum. What now?

The situation had to get worse before we finally gained a little ability to look and think about the future. Maybe that is why the merciful Lord took away our electricity, to tear me away from the news and let my brain function again. I realized that I had not left the courtyard in all the days since the war began. I had no reason to. Transportation wasn't running and so the nearby village shops were closed. Taxis wouldn't come here because their drivers were worried about the lack of fuel and about the Russian culture which our wonderful Armed Forces of Ukraine were mercilessly scorching on the Zhyto- myr Road. Conversations with our next-door neighbours did not, honestly, bring me much intellectual satisfaction. They were Russian-speaking and pro-Russian, to a certain extent, and elicited complicated feelings in me, to put it mildly. In the first days of the war even the thought of conversing with them triggered an internal resistance. I didn't want to hear their thoughts, chatter, rumours and predictions; I knew their in- adequacy all too well.

Spending time in the building and in the courtyard without leaving was only possible while we at least had certain necessi- ties like water and electricity. When they disappeared, along with the phone connection, it became clear that we wouldn't make it on our own. The first thing we needed to do was to find some water. Thank God, water had never been an issue round here. We lived next to Lake Gloria, which is huge, and there were wells in several of our cooperative's yards. We didn't know whether we could actually access them, but at least we could ask the head of the cooperative about it. We needed to meet with him and find out whether he could help us with anything.

In the afternoon I went out onto the street for the first time since the war began and started in the direction of the head's office. Many people I had never seen before were walking along the street and kids ran about, yelling and laughing. Men were smoking and women were chatting. Teenagers sat on the steps of the office and played card games. Along the road that led along Blyzhni Sady towards Nova Hreblia and further (ideally, all the way to the safety of Rivne itself), people of various ages were strolling and there was a sense that they came here to wait for victory, something that didn't seem to be imminent. I looked at them all in amazement. Who are they? Usually only three or four families lived here towards the end of winter, and I knew all of them and they knew me. I would only see the other people who owned houses here in the summer, ambling in the forests and fields and going to the lake.

Later, it turned out that lots of people had come here before the war, because they had decided that it would be much safer here than in Kyiv. Of course, they had been mistaken. The representatives of Russian ballet and exceptional Russian spirituality didn't end up taking Kyiv, though they tried several times, while here in our cottage community a real shitshow ensued.

Our village stores closed, along with those in the nearby town. People lined up for fuel at the nearest petrol station only to be dispersed by a Russian armoured personnel carrier shooting a round at the crowd. In the village closest to us, Kadyrov's people executed a family who refused to feed them. Their refusal was justified: they had a lot of kids. None of them survived. Our head told me this in a whisper. He always spoke Ukrainian and only Ukrainian, even while under occupation. The pharmacies were closed and even if they opened they wouldn't be able to stock the most basic medicines. Most people who came here would bring a few days' worth of food and medicine, if not a week's worth.

Returning home, I thought: *'You poor things'*. I could think of nothing else. When the banging got too close I was overwhelmed with pity, sadness and, of course, horror. I began to feel less afraid for myself and my wife. Our own fears looked comical alongside those who were walking the streets of our village with infants.

Right after we had lost our electricity, we began to understand that there were two Ukraines. One was big, beautiful, and to a certain extent imagined. It was compelling and we all worried about its fate in the war. We saw ourselves as a living part of it. The other Ukraine was not as dramatic but was instead concrete and present, and consisted of the people who ended up between life and death in the territory of this small cottage community known as Blyzhni Sady.

Gathering myself together, I reported once again to Mary and her son. They sanctioned us to pray for the Armed Forces of Ukraine and for strategic relations with the Pentagon, and by the next day I decided to go out and see some people. I needed to know what kind of world our little cooperative had ended up in. As I left, I ran into a commission that was making the rounds, conducting a census on the conditions of our cottage community life. The conditions turned out to be 'difficult'. Blyzhni Sady, the smallest of all the cooperatives, housed 139 people, 99 of whom were adults. We had almost a dozen women in various stages of pregnancy, a number of ill people who needed medicine at the earliest possible opportunity, including insulin, five or six infants, and a very competent territorial defence force that was nevertheless limited in its capabilities.

At 6 p.m. every evening a meeting took place, at which various issues regarding the self-defence of the cooperative would be decided. People would exchange news and the latest night-patrol unit would be assigned. The possibility of leaving the occupied territory was discussed. Most of the families had their own cars as well as fuel reserves. They discussed how to get past the Russian roadblocks and leave. But since my wife and I had neither a car nor fuel, I didn't give these conversations much weight. When I got home all I talked about was what I had heard and seen. We were so happy that our little cottage community, Ukraine, still existed, that we were not alone and that we Ukrainians were special, and particularly good at organizing ourselves under any circumstances.

But by the next morning the Great Exit began by car and by foot. I was doing my exercises and I saw cars with white flags and large signs reading 'CHILDREN' driving past our yard in the direction of the Russian roadblocks. Not one, not two, but dozens, then hundreds. The first ones who left got it the worst. They say that buried in a cemetery near our cottages in those first days was a family, a man, a woman and two kids, who were shot by the Russians at the first roadblock. I heard of others who tried to escape too, only to meet with horrific consequences. But this stopped no one.

I'll tell you something else. If my wife and I had been in possession of our own car and fuel in those days, we wouldn't have thought twice. After just a week, our sense of helplessness and doom was too strong, and the sense of our inevitable death emerging from Lake Gloria and the pine forest was too clear.

Translated by Mark Andryczyk

Hitler's War

Andriy Bondar

13 June 2022

'This is Putin's war, not Pushkin's,' Claudia Roth, the German Federal Government Commissioner for Culture and the Media, said recently, yet again repeating the mantra of culture and politics being fundamentally divided. It has become very popular recently in some Western circles. But as unoriginal and infantile as it is to try to reduce all Russian evil to just one name, the paradox lies in the fact that one can't consider Claudia Roth to be a *Putinversteher*. She comes from the ecological left and has dedicated her entire political life to defending the rights of discriminated against LGBT people, and to developing women's soccer in her own country. Her Green Party is for the most part arguably the most consistently pro-Ukrainian party in German politics. Words like these are repeated and advanced from an ideological position, one which narrows politics to processes and events only, leaving culture an exalted, sentimental superstructure freed from the nerves of national cultural dominance or imperial colonial mechanics. Culture is seen to function as if cleansed of ideology.

The minister seems to underline the importance of culture, and she obviously believes in its therapeutic value. Culture cannot be cancelled or boycotted, because it is capable of alleviating the suffering of a person or a community even in the most difficult times. That is, over here you have, separately, the politics of 'one person, who is guilty of all of this', with its world of horror, violence, and a world championship in tank biathlon* – while over there you have human spirituality expressed in texts and images: the great literature of the Tolstoyevskys, opera, ballet, figure skating, freely accessible in every corner of the world like any given and proven system, where there is both calico and brocade, as the Russian folk song has it.

By withdrawing culture from the political sphere, Roth and many like-minded individuals narrow the entire influence of culture. Culture, like a tablet of aspirin, is capable of healing that which has been damaged by politics, by its absence or passivity, that which has been devastated by 'one person, who is guilty of all this'. Russian culture has never been beyond politics. It was always by the empire's side, as its window dressing and as its creator and mastermind going back to the days of the archbishop Theofan Prokopovych in the eighteenth century. This is not evident to the European left, which always prefers to operate only within the visible tip of the iceberg, the exported myth of the breadth of the Russian soul embodied in the aesthetic arts. Nor is it evident that when speaking of Russian culture one important and fundamental aspect fails to receive attention: over the past hundred years the imperialism within their culture has never been revised. Under similarly unfavourable political conditions, other developed European cultures transformed themselves after a collapse; German culture reckoned with home-grown Nazism in the second half of the twentieth century. Yes, German culture itself: Thomas Mann, Günter Grass, Heinrich Böll and W. G. Sebald atoned

---

* Russia holds International Army Games (a sort of military Olympics), in which a major event is the tank biathlon. They seem to win it every year.

for the Germans after their catastrophe that was caused by 'one person, who is guilty of all this'. Mrs Roth doesn't understand that the Stalinist catastrophe of Solzhenitsyn's *Gulag Archipelago*, for example, or Varlam Shalamov's camp stories, reduced Stalinism to Communism and didn't even consider Russian imperialism. Russia never started the process of reckoning and failed to put a stop to its own desire to destroy the world today.

But there is another side to this ritualistic, rhetorical steering of culture away from attack. It is even more striking than the German left's misunderstanding of the role of culture in an imperial power system (see Ewa Thompson's fundamental investigation, *Imperial Knowledge: Russian Literature and Colonialism*). I have in mind the key notion of leftist thought in the second half of the twentieth century: that is, the fundamental agreement among their leading thinkers that no text exists beyond a context or, following Barthes, that no artistic or even pragmatic expression exists beyond the political sphere. And that is why a phrase like 'This is Putin's war, not Pushkin's', or 'culture beyond politics', is also an instrumental, ideological method of left-wing activists that contradicts the main foundation of Marxism and post-Marxism: that power 'is everywhere and pervades everything'.

This could be written off as illiteracy, if Mrs Roth and her fellow thinkers truly didn't know about the connection between Riefenstahl, Heidegger, Speer and Nazi ideology, or about the fundamental powerlessness of the best representatives of that culture in the face of the red-hot magma of German exceptionalism, revanchism and racism in Hitler's Germany. Culture beyond politics does not exist; politics does not exist beyond culture.

Culture in totalitarian societies is always an instrument, not a goal. The goal is to realize political objectives by any means possible. Russian culture, in the context of the war with Ukraine, like the billboard of Pushkin in occupied Kherson, is not simply a tool but the fulfilment of that culture's embedded will to dominate and oppress. The main point of the Russian war is to raise the political to the level of the imperial – cultural with its aplomb of greatness and supremacy. Without Pushkin's poems 'To the Slanderers of Russia' and 'Mazepa' there would be no Putin. In this fascinating totalitarian badminton match between politics and culture there is neither room for nor the possibility of a Ukrainian culture that is different from and independent of the culture of the metropole.

That is why when someone in the West talks about 'culture without politics' I'd like to quote Vladimir Putin himself who, way back in December 2015, said this: 'It is desirable, of course, that culture be beyond politics. Then this can *be exploited* as a bridge between nations, between countries, even when there is a deterioration in relations between them. But only if no one will attempt to *exploit* culture for political interests.'

The key verb here, surely, is *exploit*. We know this well, but for some reason the Germans don't. They try to convince us that it is not the Russian people who are guilty, only Putin. Perhaps because they are still convinced that only Hitler was guilty for Germany's catastrophe. At times perhaps they still think that way. But they won't admit it to themselves.

Translated by Mark Andryczyk

On This Side of Good and Evil

Oleksandr Boichenko

20 June 2022

I and many others have been asked repeatedly: 'What should I read during the war?' Well, even before the war – both the one in Eastern Ukraine and this full-fledged Russian invasion – I tried to avoid giving advice, because you can't say the same thing to everyone: for one person, Joyce is too easy, and for someone else, a TV programme is too complicated. It's even riskier to suggest something against the backdrop of massive military trauma: you never know how this or that text will affect a particular reader's mind, racked by pain, fear and loss.

So I don't give advice. I can only share my own experiences. On one of the first evenings of the full-scale invasion, I stared at my Polish books and automatically pulled out Leopold Tyrmand's* novel *The Evil One*. I knew my brain would not be able to handle anything new and I needed to reread something, something potentially uplifting and distracting. By the way, an abridged version of *The Man with White Eyes* in the Ukrainian translation by Maria Pryhara and Valentyn Strutynsky was released back in 1959, and at the end of 2020, on the occasion

---

* Leopold Tyrmand (1920–1985), Polish novelist and journalist, who emigrated to the United States after the Second World War.

93

of the 100th anniversary of the author's birth, a new translation appeared, supplemented and amended by Hennadyi Androschuk. I haven't been able to get either the first or the second Ukrainian editions yet, but if you'd like to read it in Ukrainian, it's available.

The Man with White Eyes is written at the intersection of everything. As Tyrmand demonstrates, everything can intersect: realism, or naturalism, is grotesquely intertwined with comics about superheroes, detective investigations (state and private) with love stories, a sharp plot with numerous lyrical digressions, the tragicomedy of cloak and dagger with newspaper reportage, and so on. The characters are scrupulously embedded in the setting of post-war Warsaw, much like Joyce's are in Dublin, thanks to whom attentive architects who have read *Ulysses* would be able to reconstruct that city. Thanks to *The Man with White Eyes* I could once again prowl through those familiar streets, city squares and courtyards in the Warsaw of my mind. I suspect that it was the prospect of taking another walk through the city where I had once gallivanted around carefree on scholarships from the Ministries of Culture of the Republic of Poland that prompted me to pull Tyrmand's novel from the shelf.

Combining the seemingly incongruous features of high and low literature, *The Man with White Eyes* was the author's only bestseller, although professional critics reacted to the way he mixed genres with arrogance. In the end Tyrmand himself felt that it wasn't his most important book, that he had written better novels and essays. He had, but there is a clue in his biography that explains why Tyrmand's claim to fame is the stunning *The Man with White Eyes*, and why it isn't *Diary-1954*, which is probably his best work, or the novel praised by Witold Gombrowicz, *Secular and Love Life* (or perhaps it should be translated as *Intimate* or *Personal Life*? In the original it is *Życie towarzyskie i uczuciowe*), or the unreservedly anti-communist *The Civilization of Communism. The Man with White Eyes* wasn't a hit because it was autobiographical, for it isn't, but Tyrmand's own fate was, in entirely different circumstances, just as stunning as the plot of his most famous novel.

The genius of the Romantic period, the writer, composer and artist E. T. A. Hoffmann, was also a Prussian bureaucrat who invented surnames for Warsaw Jews, and Tyrmand thought he must have given his family their name. His family was assimilated. At least his parents, Mieczysław and Maria, thought they were. Hitler thought otherwise, and after the German occupation of Warsaw both ended up in the Majdanek concentration camp, and Tyrmand's father died there. His mother survived and left for Israel at the first opportunity.

Before the war Tyrmand studied at the Faculty of Architecture in Paris for a year, where he perfected his French and fell headfirst in love with Western culture, jazz music in particular. Later, fleeing from the Nazis, he ended up in Vilnius, then occupied by the Soviets, and joined the staff of the newspaper *Komsomolskaya Pravda* (*The Truth of the Komsomol*), which they published in Polish. The link to the *Komsomol* didn't help him in the end: in April 1941 the NKVD* secret police were tipped off about a suspicious Polish Jew in Soviet Lithuania. By May he had been given an eight-year sentence. In June the Germans attacked the USSR and bombed a train that was carrying the captives, including Tyrmand. Whoever survived, escaped. Tyrmand returned to Vilnius, where he obtained fake French

---

* The People's Commissariat for Internal Affairs, which operated from 1917 to 1930 in the USSR and fulfilled the commands of Stalin during the purges.

documents and set off for the Third Reich, relying only on the truth that 'the darkest place to be is under a lantern.'

That turned out to be quite right. By 1944, Tyrmand had managed to live in relative safety in Mainz and Wiesbaden, Frankfurt am Main and Vienna, where he worked as a translator and railroad worker, a librarian and a waiter. One day he met a German soldier on the bank of a river. The German soldier was playing jazz records, stolen in France, on a portable record player. Always a contrarian, Tyrmand asked the soldier, 'Doesn't it bother you, a true Aryan, that Negroes and Jews are playing this?' 'No,' the true Aryan answered, 'as long as the music is good.' This they agreed on. Later on, in the late mid-1950s, Tyrmand, having become the chief promoter of 'good music' in Poland, wrote about this episode in his book *On the Shores of Jazz*.

But before that, towards the end of the war, he did eventually end up in a concentration camp. While working as a sailor on a German ship he attempted to escape to Sweden. Once he was freed he returned to Poland and began a brilliant career as a journalist, rabble-rouser and womanizer. After his novel *Secular and Love Life* was banned, he emigrated to the United States and worked out a cooperation agreement with the Parisian journal *Kultura*, but soon parted ways with the publisher Jerzy Giedroyc and his team, as he quickly turned from a desperate Eastern freethinker into an arch-Western conservative. Why? Because he saw the dominance of leftist idiots in American intellectual life as being useful for the Kremlin and concluded that only conservatism would be capable of saving America from itself. I think he was about 50 per cent right.

But all this would take place much later. Instead, let's return to the year 1953. *Tygodnik Powszechny* (*The Common Weekly*, a Catholic newspaper), where the future émigré works, refuses to publish an obituary of Stalin. In response the authorities fire the entire editorial board. So, on 1 January 1954, the unemployed Tyrmand starts work on his *Diary* and writes every day for three months. But he receives a directive from the Czytelnik Publishing House to write something criminally sensational about Warsaw hooligans. Stopping in the middle of a diary paragraph on 2 April, he proceeds to write *The Man with White Eyes*. When it was published the following year, it was a hit.

What was I looking for when I reread this novel, consciously or otherwise? To distract myself, to reassure myself. To roam around my favourite places in Warsaw and immerse myself in the cruel humour and sarcasm of language. I got all this, and something else I didn't expect, too.

In a novel, every fully realized character can become an image of an entire society. And every well-captured city can become an image of the whole world. In the world of *The Man with White Eyes*, a supposedly respectable director of a lawyer's office is in fact a despicable, cruel and arrogant gangland boss who uses his underlings to terrorize everyone around him. The protagonist confronts him and, not expecting much from the police, cracks the gangster's jaw himself. Interestingly, it is the gangland boss who gives the protagonist the nickname 'The Evil One', though the criminal boss's victims could've told you who was fighting the good fight and who wasn't. The gangland boss and the main hero had previously been accomplices and share common sins in their past. Now their paths have diverged and the crime boss can't take it because he is used to believing that the whole world should fear him; a tough guy who never faces any consequences. To the joy of readers, in the end he gets his comeuppance.

Leopold Tyrmand could never have dreamed of my inter-
pretation of his novel. But I have one piece of very simple
advice to impart about reading: during the Russian – Ukrainian
war, read anything you want. Whatever it is, it will always be
about the Russian – Ukrainian war.

Translated by Michael M. Naydan and Alla Perminova

Conveniences and Values

Andriy Bondar

29 June 2022

Our recent rendezvous with Europe was not planned by us, nor by Europe. Though perhaps it would be more accurate to say that it was predicted, but not with such scope, drama and inevitability. The millions of forced refugees who have crossed the western borders of our country are a varied group: it includes those who have already been to Europe many times, those who have visited once or twice and those who have never travelled outside their local area. There are those who can slot easily into foreign cultures and those who have had no experience of them.

To understand that world, every one of our refugees uses as much energy as is necessary to feel, if not fully comfortable, then somewhat all right there. Let's not forget, after all, that this large migration of Ukrainians to Europe was involuntary, not intentional. Those who wanted to move there either for the sake of increasing their income or simply to change where they lived (the so-called economic migrants of the past few decades) had had every opportunity to do so long before the fully fledged war began.

A 'rendezvous' of the traumatized with the healthy, emotionally stable and satiated world will often be traumatic. First, due to the language barrier, the inability to understand each other even about small things. But thankfully, Google Translate exists, and it's great that every smartphone has Duolingo, and it's wonderful that it is European people who greet us there upon arrival and not, God forbid, Russians. Ukrainians can easily understand Europeans on a basic level, and Ukrainians only travel (if they do so voluntarily) to the West, not to Russia. They end up in Russia only when they are taken there. When a person is taken somewhere against their will they lose their final scraps of freedom and become a hostage, an evildoer or a slave. Nothing will save them: not a solid knowledge of the Russian language, not money, not even the consulate in Moscow.

Europe is an *Other* for a post-Soviet person, one which slowly and unexpectedly becomes *Ours*. But before it does, the new life experience of that *Other*, with its frustrations and disappointments, pours onto our people like a cornucopia. It provokes memories that naturally elicit a thirst for conclusions, comparisons and defences.

It's understood that the first thing that our compatriot accepts is The Europe of Conveniences. And it is here that many people's 'eyes are opened'. It turns out that Ukraine has several advantages in everyday life, something that Europe either does not provide right away, or cannot provide at all, thanks to cultural differences.

Upon the old yeast of a Soviet's pride in having the best and fairest existence, stories of today's dissatisfaction with everyday life in Europe are stacked.

Suddenly and inevitably, the forced émigré realizes that The Ukraine of Conveniences is not so bad after all, and is actually better than Europe in some respects. Where else can you find city and intercity transport that is as affordable as it is here? Nowhere. This is self-evidently true: you can take the Metro for eight *hryvnias* a ride, undoubtedly the cheapest in Europe. And coffee – our café culture is so refined. Our coffee is aromatic and plentiful. Where else could you find something like it? Italy? Don't make me laugh. They don't even know what a flat white or *raf* is! Ukraine's coffee has surpassed everyone else's for decades. And dear Lord, what about our shops? Our shops are open on weekends! In Europe, you can't buy anything on the weekend. You won't be able to find an open bar. And in the Czech Republic you can die of starvation on a Sunday evening. In Austria, too. In some countries you can't have a decent lunch during the summer because they have a siesta for half a day. Just try and find a restaurant that's open over lunch in southern France or in Spain during the summer and isn't a McDonald's. Their internet is slow and they don't have WiFi everywhere like we do. Our internet is the cheapest in Europe, only seven dollars a month. And we have *Dia*, our app that allows us to share official documents on our phones. Here in Europe everyone is jealous of us because they don't have their own *Dia* and, it seems to them, they never will.

Examples of our pluses compared to their minuses can be multiplied according to experience. Everyday dissatisfaction with The Europe of Conveniences overflows with ease into a dissatisfaction with Europe in general. Within the framework of our candidacy for the European Union, it provokes a sentimental question: 'Well, why do we need Europe at all, if Ukraine is so much more convenient?'

Such an approach, brimming with pride and maudlin patriotism, would be nothing but a charming naivety if it didn't win over the hearts and minds of our people, who have temporarily been deprived of their homeland. This approach reduces Europe to nothing but conveniences, giving rise to another, more fundamental, question: 'Why then, does

Europe prosper? Why do people choose to go there and why don't they leave?'

The thing is that Europe is not just about conveniences. We long for Europe not for the sake of fast WiFi or great coffee, not even for the total digitization and robotization of industry. These things, practice has shown us, we can take care of on our own. We were even able to build an orderly system of petrol stations without the European Union, with convenient bathrooms and that boast borsch or beef soup as appetizers in the attached restaurant, with chicken Kyiv as the main course. I haven't even mentioned our internet bank, Pryvat24, or our mobile bank, Monobank.

What we need is The Europe of Values. That is what our candidacy for the EU is about, not about the ability to have borsch and chicken Kyiv at two in the afternoon under the burning southern French sun. We need a Ukraine that lives according to the European model of coexistence between people and society. We need an absence of corruption, or at least only as much as exists in Europe. We need independent courts that can't be bribed, which we aren't even close to having now. Our society needs total control over Ukraine's executive powers. Our investments must be reliably protected. We must join the general Euro-Atlantic security system, protecting us from Russian bombs for ever. Our rates of infant mortality and suicide should be close to Europe's. We must clean up our country, one that, over the years, has been turned into a giant rubbish bin. We need to establish an independent media, one that doesn't broadcast blatant pay-to-publish pieces and that acts as a buffer between big business and the government.

Finally, our education system should be reformed so that our citizens can see the difference between a world of convenience and a world of values. And we must remember one simple thing: that which is convenient for us is not necessarily convenient for others. That Europe as a united and permanent entity does not exist. That Europe has countries as different as Finland and Romania, Denmark and Greece. But that they are all united by that which we still don't know how to, or cannot, learn, but which we must: to live according to rules and laws. To respect your fellow beings. To recognize principles and hold on to them. We don't have an alternative to the EU, there is no third path. The war has confirmed this. This war is not about the fastest WiFi in the world or a prevalence of modern cafés. It is about freedom and it is about life, it's about having the same rules for everyone.

Translated by Mark Andryczyk

Empires Die Out Earlier

Taras Prokhasko

30 June 2022

My maternal grandfather's and paternal grandmother's sisters became friends almost immediately after my parents' marriage. The two older ladies became so close that even if the marriage hadn't worked out it would have been worth doing for their friendship alone.

They were both, as Jamaica the Cossack said, odd ducks.* One was born in North Carolina and experienced world war on its front lines, and knew the archbishop Sheptytsky and the painters Trush and Novakivsky. She won the hearts of the most handsome nationalists, melted tar on the roof of the Ukrainian coffee factory in Pidzamche, Lviv, prepared for the next action with the young Polish independence movement *Endecja*, and eventually went into hiding in Stanislaviv.

The other ran a guest house in Morshyn, rode her bicycle everywhere, and was sentenced to permanent internal exile in Khabarovsk Krai. (The fact that she was first sent to Chita and then eventually returned from Siberia for good most likely seriously affected her understanding of concepts like

---

* 'Jamaica the Cossack' is a poem by Yuri Andrukhovych from his 1991 collection *Ekzotychni Ptakhy i Roslyny (Exotic Birds and Plants)*, in which one of the characters is described as being 'an odd duck'.

'eternity', 'immortality', 'beyond time', 'the flow of time' and 'in two years'.)

And in their old age – back then it seemed to me that they were both old, I always saw each as being in their seventies – they decided to derive personal satisfaction from the Soviet Union, from Stalinism, Brezhnevism, the Bolsheviks, from all the NKVDs, for their not totally wasted but interrupted lives.

In a strange way they understood that the empire, which had wronged them in so many ways, was not eternal. They knew that, because everything is in God's hands and you never know when your time will be up, the empire could fool them and die early and so avoid making reparations or taking care of the basic needs of the formerly enslaved, as empires are wont to do.

Having obtained a solid education in the dialectic method and in several other fields, these grandmothers came to a simple conclusion: the biggest window of possibility within any empire comes when it has accumulated an unnaturally large variety of lands. And the greatest right of the peripheral citizen of empire is to have access not only to the metropole (which is not all that interesting because it's already been so heavily written about, with books available in the city of Zalishchyky or in the town of Dora), but to other peripheries and colonies, scattered in four directions away from the metropole.

And so it began. Every year, sometimes twice, the two friends signed up for an amazing tour (mostly via rail, which was a tourist option back then) to lands which, as they knew quite well, they would not be able to visit after the ruin of empire. A week in a Baltic province. Vilnius, Kaunas, Klaipėda, Riga, Tallinn. Or Fergana, Samarkand, Tashkent, and a view of the Tian Shan. The maze of train tracks and cities of the so-called Trans-Caucasus (Armenia wanted to emphasize its uniqueness, so it added Sevan and the expected Ararat to the route). Or to those idiotic abbreviations such as YuBK (the Southern Coast of Crimea) – they both, by the way, loved Chekhov's letters and diaries – or ChPK (the Black Sea Coast of the Caucasus), but they liked the pine trees in Pitsunda the best. There were lots of trips like that. They made it all the way to the Baikal. But not to Khabarovsk. They both loved nature and ruins. As fate would have it, there was nothing more reliable and beautiful in their lives.

And now, thinking about their journeys, a few questions come to mind. First, how did they know that they had to hurry? Second, how did they find a common language when one was born in 1900 while the other was born in 1909, which in the twentieth century was a difference the size of a canyon? Thirdly, why didn't I, a lover of nature and ruins, ever ask to join them for at least one of their expeditions? I will never be able to make up for that.

Translated by Mark Andryczyk

Why Does It Have to be Ilyich?*

Yuri Andrukhovych

1 July 2022

Kyiv is now more or less successfully being de-Russified. Or it might be better to say that it continues with all decisiveness to prepare for de-Russification. They have even proposed to rename Bulgakov Street Hulak-Artemovsky† Street. The same name that the very man who was deprived of his former presidential rank in disgrace once pronounced as Artyomovsky.‡

There are many other non-trivial proposals. I have three personal favourites. The grandfather-fabulist Krylov§ would be replaced by Matsuo Bashō (1644–1694), a brilliant Japanese poet. Fyodor Dostoyevsky (an assault on the sacred!) would be swapped with the name of the pop artist Andy Warhol, about whom a certain poet once rhetorically asked whether he was a

---

* Both the founder of the USSR, Vladimir Ilyich Lenin, and Pyotr Ilyich Tchaikovsky share the same patronymic – Ilyich (i.e. the son of Ilya). Lenin was often known just by his patronymic in the USSR – Ilyich.

† Petro Hulak-Artemovsky (1790–1865). Romantic and Sentimentalist Ukrainian poet and fabulist.

‡ This is in reference to the disgraced Ukrainian president Viktor Yanukovych, who was forced to flee Ukraine in 2014.

§ The most famous Russian fabulist, Ivan Krylov (1769–1844).

Rusyn or a *khokhol*.* The communizing and pro-Soviet to the point of obscenity Romain Rolland would be replaced by another Frenchman, not a pro-Soviet one, but the inventor of science fiction and discoverer of mysterious islands, Jules Verne, to whom I have given my personal gratitude since childhood.

It has got to the point that I no longer know which of the streets I would most prefer to live on – Bashō, Warhol or Jules Verne.

But streets are streets, and city squares are city squares. On the other hand, the National Music Academy of Ukraine, or more precisely its leadership, does not want to submit to the trend and is striving to retain its name of Petr Ilyich Tchaikovsky at all costs. Instead, among the rebellious lower echelons of the music conservatory (and this doesn't only include students), the opposite idea predominates: there is no place for Tchaikovsky here. The students are complaining that their opinions are 'brazenly ignored', and even that 'threats from the former adviser to the rector' have been made.

The topic of this renaming (or rather its absence) has, as they say, stirred me, which is why I will permit myself some further contemplation of the subject.

Tchaikovsky is of course a first-class musical giant and inarguable classic. Inarguable to the extent that the very phrase 'classical music' evokes his name. And how many times have I,

* A poem by the Ukrainian poet Petro Midyanka, which was turned into a popular song by the rock band Plach Yeremiyi (Jeremiah's Cry). Rusyns (also called Ruthenians or Carpatho-Rusyns) are a Slavic ethnic group that is spread across several Central and East European countries. *Khokhol* is a Russian pejorative for a Ukrainian.

after setting my receiver to the frequency of some Classic FM station in the so-called distant abroad, come upon the whisper-soft voice of a presenter, who up to a hundred times a day tirelessly (and even more whisper-softly) utters the name of the enduring Pyotr Ilyich Tchaikovsky? If classical music has its own pop hits, then Tchaikovsky is the indisputable leader, and pieces from *The Nutcracker* and *Swan Lake* are invariably always in the top ten. A certain American musicologist quite correctly summed up Tchaikovsky's creative legacy as 'a sweet, light and easy, extremely sensual, treasure house of melodies'. In other words, even those who usually struggle to stay awake at concerts of serious music can listen to Tchaikovsky with a certain amount of pleasure ('lightly and easily').

But is this enough for the National Music Academy of Ukraine to bear his name? There would have to be some other absolutely convincing reason, preferably more than one. For if it is only about genius, then the Academy might as well bear the names of Mozart or Beethoven, Verdi or Gounod, Bruckner or Wagner, Brahms or Liszt . . .

Only for some reason it does not bear their names. *For some reason*, it's Tchaikovsky!

By the way, there is also Ferenc (Franz) Liszt. In 1847, while travelling through Ukraine, he gave concerts in Kyiv and dozens of other cities, including Lviv, Chernivtsi, Kremenets, Odesa, Mykolaiv and Berdychiv. His symphonic long poem *Mazepa*,* in contrast to Tchaikovsky's opera by the same name, gives a Byronic treatment to the hero, a significantly more attractive approach than Pushkin's. In Liszt's

---

* Ivan Mazepa (1639–1709), Hetman of Ukraine from 1687 to 1709, whose Zaporozhian Host established an alliance with Sweden in the Russo-Swedish War of 1708–9.

imagination Mazepa is the embodiment of an unconquerable thirst for freedom. Liszt sensed this in Ukrainians too, even during that seemingly hopelessly-strangled-by slavery time of Nicholas I's Russia.

Liszt does not have something that Tchaikovsky supposedly does – Ukrainian roots. But for Tchaikovsky it is really 'Little Russian'* roots. His Kozak† grandfather, although he studied at the Kyiv Mohyla Academy‡ and changed his name from Chaika§ to Tchaikovsky, nevertheless served the tsar and fatherland so zealously that he was elevated to the post of mayor in Glazov in the Vyatka region of Russia. He was later registered among the nobles of the Kazan province. Frankly speaking, Tchaikovsky's grandfather Petro Chaika is a rather symbolic example of the 'right kind of *khokhol*' and isn't a bad argument for the theory of the 'imperial' role Ukrainians played in the construction of tsarist Russia.

So, Tchaikovsky willingly arranged Ukrainian melodies and sometimes based his works on Ukrainian themes – such as in *Cherevichki* (*The Tsarina's Slippers*) or the previously mentioned *Mazepa*. Is that enough?

No way, not if we take into consideration that he wrote in a

* The historically pejorative colonial name that Russia had for Ukraine and Ukrainians.
† We use the original Ukrainian name for the Ukrainian warriors instead of the colonial Russian name in English – Cossacks.
‡ Founded in 1632 by Petro Mohyla, the Academy was a leading centre of higher learning in the seventeenth and eighteenth centuries.
§ Chaika was a common last name for Ukrainian Kozaks. It means 'seagull' as well as the name of Kozak transport dugout boats that held about twenty Kozak warriors. For an image of one of the boats see the following site: https://1news.com.ua/tsikave/na-spravzhnij-kozaczkij-chajczi-vyrushyly-v-pohid-ponad-20-zaporizkyh-kozakiv.html.

letter to Nadezhda von Meck, the person closest to him:* 'I am Russian in the most complete meaning of this word.' It didn't take long for me to find this quote: over the past few years Russian propaganda has been spreading it all over the place.

Now we can argue what this 'most complete meaning' meant exactly, what it entailed. Maybe, in Tchaikovsky's understanding, his 'most complete Russianness' included his Little Russian heritage, that it was an essential part of his identity. Perhaps 'Little Russian' was one of the lower steps on the path of evolutionary movement to a greater and single *Rusian*† nationality.

But let me not overstep. I will return to more obvious things.

In my view, there are at least three reasons for renaming the Conservatory:

1) Kyiv Conservatory received the name 'Tchaikovsky' in 1940 on the centenary of his birth. This happened two years after the Conservatory was awarded the Order of Lenin on its 25th anniversary. The great leader and father of peoples *was pleased* and this was the way he showed it. In other words, the Conservatory being named after P. I. Tchaikovsky is an obvious legacy of Stalinism.

2) Looking at this phenomenon in a slightly broader context: P. I. Tchaikovsky was a favourite and active figure in Soviet cultural policy. By an irony of fate (or, rather, history) it was to the soundtrack of *Swan Lake* that the Soviet Union

---

* Nadezhda von Meck (1831–1894) was a Russian businesswoman and patron of the arts who financially supported Tchaikovsky, giving him time to write his musical compositions.

† The author is playing here with the notion of Kyivan Rus (from the eighth to twelfth centuries), from which Muscovy somewhat ironically takes the latter half of the name as the origin for the name of Russia and Russians.

strove to renew its beloved state of emergency on the first day of the August putsch. The preservation of Tchaikovsky's name may indicate a general will, conscious and subconscious, to preserve the Soviet cultural and political paradigm. But the Conservatory is not a cannery.*

3) Such an institution as the National (!) Academy of Music of Ukraine (!) should bear a name that is significant to Ukrainian musical culture. Tchaikovsky's Ukrainian origin is not enough here, nor in this instance is his successful stylization of Ukrainian folk melodies. That he was a deeply moved visitor of landlords' estates in the 'Little Russian' idyllic heartland is not enough either, nor even his lengthy stays in 'the mother of Russian cities' (Kyiv).†

Tchaikovsky has not done enough to have his name here.

And Lysenko,‡ although he would be just right, is already here in Ukraine, in Lviv.

So, shouldn't we think of someone else? How about Wedel?§ Berezovsky?¶ What about the author of the first national opera, the nephew,** by the way, of the very same Hulak-Artemovsky mentioned earlier?

---

* The author's play on the sound similarity of the two words here is untranslatable: *konservtoriya* (music conservatory) and *konservnyi zavod* (literally meaning a 'conserving' factory, i.e., a cannery where food products are conserved).

† What Russians have in the past called the capital city of Kyiv in Ukraine.

‡ The Ukrainian composer and ethno-musicologist Mykola Lysenko (1842–1912). The Mykola Lysenko Lviv National Music Academy is named after him.

§ Artem Wedel (1767–1808) was a composer of military and liturgical works.

¶ Maxim Berezovsky (1745–1777) was a composer and opera singer.

** Semen Hulak-Artemovsky (1813–1873) was a composer and musical performer and the nephew of the previously mentioned poet Petro Hulak-Artemovsky.

And does it have to be a composer? How about another prominent musical activist? For example, Oleksandr Koshyts?*

Or how about Leontovych?† How useful and pleasant it would be to tell all the unenlightened in the world that our Kyiv National Music Academy forever echoes with the genius of 'Carol of the Bells'!

Translated by Michael M. Naydan and Alla Perminova

---

* Koshyts (1875–1944), is also sometimes spelled Koshetz in English, was a composer, musicologist, and choir director, who eventually emigrated to Canada.
† Mykola Leontovych (1877–1921) was a composer of Ukrainian folklore-inspired choral works and musicologist. He composed and did the choral arrangement for what is known throughout the world as 'Carol of the Bells'.

War Diary: The Fourth Month of February

Olena Stiazhkina

7 July 2022

Kyiv, 2 June 2022

My biological father, who lives in Leningrad, sent me a picture congratulating me on the Feast of the Ascension. Only a month before, I had asked him not to attend that damned sect of the Moscow Orthodox Church. But I just quietly deleted it. Requests or explanations make no sense now.

I can't delete or block his number. Not because I don't know how. I am just unable to do it. Cancelling Pushkin and Great Russian Culture turned out to be much easier than deleting the person who spent his sperm for me, with whom I shared five years of life and who has many good – really good – deeds and intentions. On the other hand, I have an answer to Mr Taras Bulba's question in Gogol's novel: 'Well, son, have your *Lyakhs* helped you?'

Yes. Mine, ours. It is the *Lyakhs*, the Poles. They have helped and will continue to help.

And I am a daughter, not a son. But that detail is not essential.

Kyiv, 5 June 2022

'Can you find someone who will officially sign a lease for an apartment with me?'

'Come and live with us, there's no problem. We'll all fit.'

'Is this yours or a rental?'

'A rental.'

'It's not suitable. By the way, we have somewhere to live. We even have room for you. What I need is a piece of paper with a stamp that says: proper living conditions.'

'I'll try to find one. Can you wait till evening?'

Trust is when you don't ask why. You just do it, because you know: if they're asking you, they're already so up to their neck that it needs to be done quickly, yesterday, that it's a question of life, death, or both. As a rule, both.

Trust is when they tell you if they have the strength, if there is ever a right time to say that. But if they don't tell you, nothing will change. That also is trust.

She'll say afterwards, when the piece of paper certifying proper living conditions and a pile of others, just as impossibly important, will already have gone to the appropriate agencies.

Kyiv, 11 June 2022

Tomorrow is my friend's birthday. She would have been fifty-four. She stayed in Donetsk; she died in Donetsk. She gave instructions that she shouldn't be buried in a land raped by the Orcs,* but that her body should be transformed into dust or

---

* The Ukrainian pejorative name for brutal Russian soldiers. The name has its origin in Tolkien's Orcs, who are mindless brutes.

ashes. At this point she always used to laugh. She used to say she couldn't choose, but she liked ashes better. 'At least I know what I'll look like. Not very good, to be honest. Grey isn't becoming for me . . . But the dust, that's somehow not modern at all.'

She instructed that her ashes be released into the wind, over the Sea of Azov in Mariupol.

She is now somewhere over there in the wind and water, on a small cloud, over a dead city that definitely doesn't suit her, my blazing, fearless friend.

It's not her way. And everything that was not her way for dirt bags always ended up shitty.

I know for certain that Mariupol will be freed. There, in the rains and snows, in all the rivers and streams that flow into the sea in which she is now living, is my friend. Inna. Isya.

All of our dead are living there, all those who had no choice to live, as dust, ashes, or bodies in the ground.

The hell waiting for the Russians will be eternal.

Kyiv, 13 June 2022

A German historian said that Ukrainians fight with irony and elegantly. I understand what he means: our desperate jokes, memes, caricatures, songs, graduation pictures on the ruins of our schools.

But I'm not sure that I can allow him to speak like that.

Inscribing 'she died with irony and elegantly' on my grave is more or less OK. At least it's not tasteless.

But the deaths of Ukrainian soldiers and civilians. Where the hell is the irony in that? What the fuck elegance is there?

There is an epidemic of the Merkel virus among the Germans: it's as though everything is all right, but really everything is totally awful.

Kyiv, 16 June 2022

She says, 'You know, when my oldest boy left for the front, I knew how it might turn out. My chances of seeing him alive again were fifty-fifty. I expected him to die. From the very first day I knew where he would be if he didn't come back. I had a place. A terrible, dark damp place for me and a radiant, warm one for him. I didn't know exactly what it would be like. But it would be warm and radiant. A place where everything would be OK for him. Where it's good for him now . . . my youngest son died under ruins. And I scream. I scream and keep screaming. Nobody hears me, and my voice disappears. I don't have a place for him any more. I just see him there, in a basement, where he believed me that everything would be OK. I just keep screaming.'

'Yes, we'll hide it, but let's count it one more time. Don't pull it out so that people can see it! Count it in your handbag. Then we'll put it in my bra; 91 times 50 will be 4,050. Is that right?'

'It seems so.'

'Then, here, one more time, check: 91 times 50 . . . 4,050. Right?'

'It seems so . . .'

'That's all! That's it, girls, we've shitted away 500 euros. The train is leaving now, and on the border there's a jeep. We're 500 euros short! That's it! What do we do now? Call, look, so they pass it to us. In cash! Otherwise our jeep will be taken to another unit right under our nose. Oh, well, what do we do, girls?'

'Learn maths in school,' the conductor grumbles. 'You didn't shit away your money; 91 times 50 will be 4,550. Get in, or I'll call your teacher.'

Kyiv, 21 June 2022

'Instead of saying his first word, our baby makes air-raid siren sounds. Exactly – note for note. From quiet to loud, then to quiet again, and again to loud. After the war I'll enrol him in music school. I can already hear – he's got a talent.'

'Yesterday I rummaged for a medical card in my go-bag and there was a bag of crackers on top. I asked, "Who put them there?" The children responded in chorus, "We did!" I asked, "Why? We have everything!" They answered: "On the 23rd, they had everything in Irpin, too, and then it all disappeared."

The boys are seven and nine, they only spent four days in the basement. I thought they didn't even have time to get scared . . .'

She is five and he is five, too. They're playing in the park, it looks like love. She says to him, 'Will you give me all your most expensive things?' He answers: 'You're some kind of Russian. I'm not going to play with you.'

Kyiv, 23 June 2022

A Russian Nobel Peace Prize winner* sold his medal for $100.3 million. He announced that he would spend it on helping child refugees from Ukraine.

Then, after our Victory, the children will ask, why didn't he give it to the army? And I'll tell them: 'He's Russian. A liberal. An intellectual. Maybe he's a fan of a book about Ostap Bender . . .'†

No, I won't say anything about Ostap Bender and *The Twelve Chairs*. Who will read or remember this then? But the plot is good: 'We helped the children.'

Kyiv, 25 June 2022

The notifications on my phone are stuck. 'How are you?' is frozen on there. Every ten days or so I send them again. Then again. And yet . . .

Sometimes they come to life with a call or a text. But more are frozen now. Each new one is like jumping off a cliff, not knowing for sure what lies below, stones or water.

Today I wrote 'How are you?' to the Zhytomyr region, which was shelled from 4 a.m. from so-called brotherly Belarus.

---

* Dmitry Muratov, the editor-in-chief of *Novaya Gazeta*, an opposition Russian online newspaper that was shut down by Putin's regime following the Russian attack on Ukraine.
† The hero of Soviet-period comic writers Ilya Ilf and Evgeny Petrov in the novels *The Twelve Chairs* and *The Golden Calf*.

'Oy,' the phone snapped back.

'Everything is OK.'

'Everything in general is very good. Check your email. I just sent you a message.'

I read the message and am cutting and pasting it here: 'Hurray! They hit my apartment. The window, the wall of the kitchen, furniture, dishes, the door (to the water closet and to the bathroom as well. I have long wanted to combine them into one room) are missing. We were in a bomb shelter. But all the same, "Hurray!" Don't worry, they didn't hit my head. Read carefully: I was in a bomb shelter. I went up to my apartment at noon. Our gas is still running. We still have water, but why "Hurray", you might be asking? They didn't hit their target! They were aiming for a military unit and warehouses, where our people were, along with Western military equipment. The rocket's flight got cut short.

'Just imagine! Everything survived. Everyone is alive. Only my kitchen is damaged! So, how are you?'

Kyiv, 26 June 2022

Our dog Kulli jumped onto the bed, pulled the blanket over herself, bit my daughter on the leg and dragged her to the hallway. Her hind legs were trembling. Her head was spinning and her neck was stretched straight as a cord. Kulli guided the entire family out into the corridor. She herself went to the bathroom, lay down under the sink and waited quietly for the end of the air-raid siren.

In the morning, four rockets landed half a kilometre away. Kulli is a dog from Bucha. She knows how to hide in the right way, how long to wait, and when to come out.

Given how zealously she tried to save us, Kulli has acknowledged that we are her family now.

Kyiv, 29 June 2022

Announcements, new and old, are pasted on the door of an apartment building in the Obolon district, Kyiv. Among the new ones are an advertisement for water and seedlings delivery, phone numbers for the hotline for missing persons, a request to pay for the house intercom phone system, and a message about shutting off hot water. From the old ones, in nearly washed-away letters, is the following: 'The door slamming is like an explosion.'

It could be the beginning of a poem. Maybe it was a poem. Only I don't know what the second line should be: 'The door slamming is like an explosion, there is no need for commotion.' Or 'The door slamming is like a bomb. If you hear it, don't worry, we've not gone.'

Translated by Michael M. Naydan and Alla Perminova

Simplicity

Sophia Andrukhovych

14 July 2022

The first thing we encounter in Lisbon is a rally in support of the Azov Regiment, which is being held captive by the Russians.* People gather in the Praça do Comércio next to the stone king José, his horse trampling snakes with its hooves. From weak speakers a cycle of four or five songs can be heard (Khlyvniuk's version of 'Chervona Kalyna', something by Okean Elzy, an ode to Mariupol, and a few other patriotic tunes), but they're experiencing technical issues and each of them plays for about thirty seconds, then stops and gives way to the next one. More and more people arrive. Those who stay are Ukrainians wrapped in blue and yellow flags, dressed in embroidered shirts, or holding placards bearing photos of the Azov soldiers. Locals and tourists stop with interest, read the texts on the placards, listen to the music and, eventually, move on.

'Are you from Ukraine?' a stocky man asks me. 'What are

* The Azov Regiment was founded in 2014 as a volunteer paramilitary militia to fight pro-Russian forces in the Donbas. Later, it became part of the National Guard of Ukraine and defended the city of Mariupol from Russian attack in 2022. After sheltering, along with civilians, in the Azovstal iron and steel works complex for weeks, the regiment surrendered and were taken to Russian-controlled territory where they became prisoners of war.

you doing here?' He is attempting to extend the practice of getting acquainted. Then he pokes me with his hand, holding a large fried sardine sandwich wrapped in several layers of napkins, and squints his eyes: 'Small business?'

It turns out that it is he who has been involved with small businesses in Lisbon for several years. He doesn't tell me what kind. The conversation quickly turns to war. 'I'm going back to Ukraine in a few days,' he tells me, eagerly searching my eyes for a reaction. 'But I really don't know what to do. I could be issued a draft card, you know?' I tell him that I do. He remains silent for a while. He continues, 'Well, maybe I'll join the army voluntarily. Maybe I'll go right away, when I get home. I'm a bit scared, though.' The wrinkles around his eyes deepen and his eyes are lost, childlike. 'Do you get it?' he asks me, peering at me. 'They could send me to who knows where and a bomb could get me. How do I know what's going to happen? You know? I'm scared. But I'm going in a few days. Maybe tomorrow. What should I do? Should I go or shouldn't I?' The stranger is waving around a sardine sandwich in Lisbon's Commercial Square. A pre-teen's bearded terrier happily plops onto the damp pebble in front of us. 'I can't answer that,' I reply, apologetically. 'That's your decision.'

Along with everything else this war has brought us, we find ourselves tangled in snarls of moral questions ever more tightly. They come up particularly when you cross the Ukrainian border and head west, when you see the normal, colourful life of Western Europeans compared to Ukrainians. You feel that your entire trip across Europe is really a journey through a Ukraine that has splashed over its damaged and ruined shores, through Ukrainian material that has leaked from its casing and has spread over the entire world. Now you are travelling through questions that have no answers, through reproaches of sensibilities, through hesitation and fretting, through incomplete variants of choices, each of which is worse than the last. You are travelling to a place where countless fellow citizens are suffering, lost and confused, detached from any foundation. This is what you notice first, not the astonishingly beautiful tiles on the Lisbon buildings, like seashells, not the colour of the ocean at the westernmost point of Europe, the Cabo da Roca, not the power of the winds above the Atlantic, not the flowering yellow water lilies on the Guadiana river, not the Spanish mills and small stone castles, not donkeys by the Chambray-lès-Tours, and not the family of wild boars next to the forest near Jelenia Góra.

You can see all of this and more thanks to the president of New Guinea, whose plane lands awkwardly at Lisbon airport just as you are supposed to fly out. Dozens of flights are cancelled because of the damaged airstrip and a stranger from Odesa agrees to put you up in her home, where her mother, daughter and a dog already live. And that's another habit that, in a short amount of time, became as natural as breathing for so many people in the world: doing something for someone else without hesitation. Not wasting time on analysis, doubt, or becoming choked by your own love of others: you, stranger, don't have a place to stay? Stay with us, there is still room in the kitchen, we have a comfortable cot.

The next day, my hostess Maria brings me to a party in Lisbon's industrial district, close to the Tagus river. Inspired hipsters talk about how they share solar energy and show the guests the thing they are most proud of, three types of basil that they grow in gigantic white cubes, on cork made of coconut crumbs. A young tour guide lovingly shows us the eco-friendly growing systems that water the bulbs. Guests are offered basil pesto sandwiches, pizza with fresh tomatoes and basil, a cocktail made of rum and basil water, and two different kinds of basil kombucha. These quirks seem so wholesome: I feel like I have gone mad and in my delirium have ended up in Paradise, where people have nothing better to do than taste-test different types of basil.

I notice that I am checking the news in Ukraine more often than usual, and when it doesn't get updated for a while I reread the same articles two or three times.

Human consciousness is a flexible and powerful phenomenon, but when it is forced to integrate despair about people dying in a Kremenchuk shopping centre amidst ashes and smoke beneath fortified concrete structures with basil growing coolly and silently on snow-white posts, it begins to deform, as if being eaten away by something acrid and deadly.

Are these deformed regions of consciousness obstacles that emerge between a person and the surrounding world or are they a magnifying glass, a means of getting into the very core of difficult-to-reach levels of existence? Or are they the only means of reaching the parallel world of another person, the part which is usually inaccessible?

For three days and three nights I ride in a bus across Europe, heading east from its most western point. It is impossible not to run into Ukrainians on the road, on public transport or in train stations and roadside cafés these days. They are recognizable right away, they don't even try to hide.

They are touching, vulnerable, disoriented and frightened. They are gapingly sensitive. But they can also be dirty, disrespectful, loud and outspoken. You want to protect, shelter, embrace them. You want to help them, but at the same time they scare you, you feel shame and indignation. These are people from your country, these are your people; you inevitably associate yourself with them. More than once you cringe like a coward and turn away, amazed at how the locals are able to be so patient and tolerant. Could they, those Ukrainians who have fled the war, be different? Surely you are aware that there are so many others, but it is these, the excessive and discrepant, that draw the most attention. What have they been forced to endure? Did the war make them like this?

There is one young woman who can be heard a hundred metres away from the bus. She gesticulates wildly and, upon entering the bus, seems to fill it entirely with her being. She is incapable of restraining her emotions, thoughts and impulses within herself. Our bus is travelling through Germany, but she appeals to her fellow passengers in her Russian language, compensating for her lack of knowledge of foreign words with loudness, pitch and staring. Those who can understand her quickly learn that this is the first time in her thirty-six-year life that she has had to leave her village in south-eastern Ukraine. They have always got along with the Russians, and now this is happening, it is delusion and insanity, and they can't understand the reason for it. The woman describes a bombed school and her neighbour, an eleven-year-old girl, who perished under her own collapsed building. The woman sprinkles her monologues with 'ja pierdolę (Polish for 'holy shit'; apparently she does know a few foreign words), and when she finally notices Polish-language signs on storefronts outside she falls into a dangerous ecstasy. She starts kissing the woman wearing glasses sitting next to her. 'I can understand!' she exclaims in a hoarse voice. 'I can read in Polish! I didn't even know I had learned to read. I can understand! Oh God. Poland! Dear ones, ours!'

Her happy hysterics become the reason for the rest of my conversation with the woman sitting next to me. We look at each other, embarrassed and scared, unsure whether our illustrious fellow traveller is in need of our assistance. It turned out that the woman next to me was from Dnipro and had already been living in Switzerland for some time. But her daughter had quickly had enough: 'This isn't life,' she had told her mother, and she returned home to her husband, who was a volunteer. 'I spoke with her today,' the woman said. 'There have already been four fly-bys since morning. At first they sat in the corridor but now they've gone out for a walk because it's impossible to live cowering.' Later she begins to talk about the loneliness she lives with now. 'Not a day goes by that I don't think about how great our life was before,' she sighs bitterly. 'I travelled a lot back then, too. But I always knew that I only ever wanted to live in Ukraine.'

In the middle of the night, on the Ukrainian–Polish border, I overhear a conversation between women I can't see. 'From where are you returning?' one asks in Russian. 'From Italy,' the other responds in a western Ukrainian accent. 'Who hosted you there?' 'Well, I just went on holiday with my child. On all kinds of trips,' the other responds offhandedly. The first woman is perplexed. She stays silent for a while. And then without any segue begins to talk emotionally about the dormitory in which she was settled in Poland and about the shame she will endure due to the badly behaved and thankless children there, who trashed and destroyed, littered and wrecked everything. 'There are all kinds of kids,' the other woman tries to say. 'No,' the first woman categorically cuts her off. 'They're all the same. And their parents are all the same. They have no conscience. They just don't care. I don't know how our hosts put up with this.'

At daybreak we can see that our bus is travelling under strings of milky-white clouds, gently extending outwards on the endless horizon. A young student sitting in front of me dreamily rests her forehead on the window. The day before, she had told her mother about her favourite professor's lessons on the history of Europe, explained the Israeli–Palestinian conflict, and watched a documentary about a diver who comes to love an octopus. She read poems by an English poet, translating the lines that moved her the most for her mother. *'And when I make it through the foulest challenges, when I have eaten the shame of my own ineptitude, when I've lost that which I did not have, I will obtain complete simplicity, as if I had never existed, and then I will have arrived.'* 'Simplicity?' the mother asks, doubtful. The girl hesitates: 'Well, it's English. You can translate it many different ways. The word is simplicity – our *prostota*'.

We are finally in Ukrainian territory and the virtuous morning sun uncovers the girl's impressionability and beauty. She yawns and reveals to her mother: 'In those woods I came to understand that I really do love my life.'

Translated by Mark Andryczyk

Letters from and to the Sultan

Yuri Andrukhovych

15 July 2022

In 1676 the Sultan of the Ottoman Porte sent the autonomous Zaporozhian army a letter inviting (or, rather, telling) them to submit to his rule. There was nothing exotic in this gesture: throughout their history the Kozaks had repeatedly taken the side of the Turks against the Poles, as well as that of the Poles against the Turks. Which is why the Sultan wanted them at the beck and call of his long fingers. Maybe that would solve the 'Kozak question' once and for all.

Two hundred and thirty or so years later this historical episode prompted the creation of one of the most representative poems of new French, and therefore world, poetry.

But Guillaume Apollinaire's 'Answers of the Zaporozhian Kozaks to the Sultan of Constantinople' wouldn't have ever been written if something else hadn't preceded it: the legendary answer from the Kozaks to the Sultan. Apollinaire created his fifteen-line masterpiece around it. In his confused search for his own genealogy (there was no one he didn't call his ancestors), Apollinaire sometimes mentioned the Zaporozhian Kozaks. There were moments when he considered himself a direct descendant of Napoleon, the pope in Rome, the richest Jewish banker in the world and also, perhaps, the Chief Hetman of the Ukrainian Kozaks, Sirko.

In other words, Apollinaire was sometimes drawn to the southern Ukrainian steppes. One can see his *Calligrammes* as a continuation of the graphic poems of the archpriest Ivan Velychkovsky, the greatest futurist of the Ukrainian baroque period.

But let's return to the Kozaks.

In their reply to the Sultan, dated 1676, these rabble-rousers and, I might say, knights of the steppe, rejected any kind of formal respectfulness and, it seems, penned the following:

You are a Turkish demon, a brother and friend of the damn devil, the secretary of Lucifer himself! What the hell kind of knight are you that you can't kill a hedgehog with your bare ass? The devil shits and your army devours it. You will not have Christian sons beneath you. We do not fear your army. We will battle with you on land and on water. You are a Babylonian cook, a Macedonian wheelwright, a Jerusalem brewer, an Alexandrian goatherd, a Great and Little Egyptian swineherd, an Armenian pig, a Tatar quiver, a Kamyanets executioner, a Podolian thief, the jester of the world and underworld, the grandson of a viper, the hook of our cock and fool of our God. A pig's snout, a mare's ass, a slaughterhouse dog, an unbaptized forehead, fuck your mother! This is the answer of the Kozaks to you, filth. You are unworthy of the mother of Christ. We don't know the date, because we don't have a calendar, the month is in the sky,* the year is in the book, and the day is the same as yours, kiss our arses!

I say that 'it seems' as the original letter has never been found. A single copy has survived, supposedly copied by hand

---

* The word for month and moon is the same in Ukrainian: *misiats'*.

in the 1870s from the original and published in Russia at the end of the nineteenth century. The letter gained considerable popularity thanks to Ilya Repin's historical painting *Reply of the Zaporozhian Cossacks*. The artist worked on it for eleven years, from 1880 to 1891, not for nothing: its countless reproductions have decorated patriotic Ukrainians' homes for over a century.

Was Apollinaire familiar with Repin's painting? We can assume that it became the stimulus for his 'Answers', for Apollinaire and visual art are inseparable. Who hasn't written about his links to Cubism? But Repin is not Picasso and is not Braque. Repin was one of the pillars of the Russian realist artists' group The Itinerants, from which Apollinaire is rather distant aesthetically. But in this case, it is not about the aesthetic effect of the painting, but rather its informational effect. Having seen it, Apollinaire could have become interested in its historical background and sought a translation of the Kozaks' letter (his distant ancestors, it seems). The text of his poem shows that he undoubtedly read the letter.

Mykola Lukash translated Apollinaire's poetry into Ukrainian. In 1984, when I returned from the army (not the Zaporozhian one, unfortunately, but the Soviet one), you could still find a Ukrainian volume of Apollinaire in our bookshops, in the cult series *Pearls of World Lyrical Poetry*. That book was special to me. In the years after reading it, it influenced me to write the kind of poems I wrote back then.

Mykola Lukash is the saint of literary translation. There have been only a handful of people like him on this planet. He translated from fourteen languages. He had an extremely expressive voice. He wasn't a dull labourer of translation, he was a daring adventurer. His translations are incredibly alluring, you want to read them aloud to your friends. I will never forget the writer Yuri Izdrik reading me Lukash's translation of *Ball at the Opera*. I will always remember how the poet Viktor Neborak read from Lukash's translation of *Don Quixote*.

Mykola Lukash was a blessing for the Ukrainian language, he was its crown, a fact that didn't save him from a life of near starvation, his publications being banned, and political harassment. At the beginning of the 1970s, Lukash wrote a letter to the leadership of the Communist Party of Soviet Ukraine asking to be imprisoned instead of the political dissident Ivan Dzyuba, because Dzyuba had tuberculosis and might not survive his term. From that moment on he fell under the aggressive hostility of the System.

His translation of Apollinaire, officially published in 1984, must have seemed to portend a softening, given that the System was allowing him to publish again. Unfortunately, he would die fewer than four years later.

Lukash's translation of the 'Answers' is congenial: free when it comes to the letter, but strikingly exact when it comes to the spirit. Jaunting, energetic, and rowdy, as it should be.

There is a very interesting effect in reverse translation. If Apollinaire's poem is a French reflection of the Ukrainian original of the Kozak letter, then Lukash's translation is a reflection of this reflection, the Ukrainian of the French. One dreams of a French translator, a genius who could translate Lukash's Ukrainian translation back into French. There should be no end to the mirroring.

Translated by Michael M. Naydan and Alla Perminova

A Hysterical Imperial Louse

Oleksandr Boichenko

18 July 2022

I am not overly concerned with the creative legacy of Joseph Brodsky, either in general or in Ukraine, but I promised to consider it and so I must, even if Zuckerberg's artificial intelligence will find hate speech in my words. That's an interesting accusation, by the way: hate speech. Because it seems to me that one of the main purposes of language is to adequately express human emotions. You feel love and you say words of love, tenderness, gratitude, and so on. But how should you express hatred, according to Zuckerberg's artificial thought? With cruise missiles, but in silence? Or better yet, with cruise missiles seasoned with words of love? Would that break the rules?

Perhaps there was a time when I believed that an eminent poet, no matter how convincingly he demonstrated his hysterical imperial essence, should not be called a louse, not literally or figuratively. Not in the sense of parasitic insect, nor in the sense of a contemptible person who has decided that he is not a 'trembling creature' but that he 'has the right', in Dostoyevsky's words. But then I read a conversation between Adam Michnik and Brodsky in which Brodsky, having heard Michnik mention the name of the eminent writer Milan Kundera, erupted in his characteristic manner: 'Kundera is a louse. A stupid Czech louse.' But isn't that the very conduct of a louse?

Couldn't Brodsky's poem 'On the Independence of Ukraine' only have been written by a parasitic insect?

We'll get to what Kundera did to Brodsky in a minute, but, for now, here's a little about the playwright Sławomir Mrożek and the writer Oksana Zabuzhko. Having just emigrated in 1963 from Poland to the West (to Italy, and then France; the US and Mexico came after), Mrożek worked on his very long, for him, story *Moniza Clavier*. The protagonist of this story ends up in Venice and by chance becomes acquainted with several representatives of the *beau monde*, but intuits that to say he is a Pole or someone from one of the small, irrelevant Central European countries would be a fatal mistake. So he only gives hints as to his homeland: the East, steppe landscapes, oriental motifs and missing teeth, and as a result the *beau monde* thinks he is Russian.

Then things started looking up: 'Transforming into a Russian, I obtained the form I was missing . . . that which up until now had been considered irreverence now transformed into extravagance. That which was hysterical magically transformed into the wonderful, unanticipated fantasy of a person truly from the East. Weakness turned into strength, stubborn tactlessness into a proud slap in the face delivered by a wide, strong hand.' Realizing how convenient this was, he conducted himself with increasing confidence, won over the growing affections of the Western upper class with his crass pranks, and soon had the love of a leading film star. This is logical: if this is how the West imagines the mysterious Russian soul, then let them masochistically enjoy it to the fullest.

As a counterpoint to *Moniza Clavier* I think about the Oksana Zabuzhko essay 'Farewell to Empire: A Few Strokes to a Portrait' published in the periodical *Dukh i Litera* soon after Brodsky's death. Writing about the giddy reverence the

Boston community shows to Great Russian Culture, Zab-uzhko says that Brodsky got away with many essentially Soviet-style transgressions that would have immediately ruined the reputation and career of any Eastern European and Third World individual with an equally traumatic past. Poles or Lithuanians (I won't even mention Ukrainians) would have to (and still have to) be 'nice' to the infantile Western elites, whereas Brodsky, who was overjoyed with the devout ecstasy of his fans, could arrive late and not ask for forgiveness, could cancel his own poetry readings and could deride his students, saying that they were 'stupid American morons and bump-kins, lacking even the most basic knowledge of literature'. Isn't this like Mrożek's portrait of the protagonist of *Moniza Clavier*, and his Venice circle in particular?

So why did the hysterical louse Joseph Brodsky call Milan Kundera a stupid Czech louse? Did he behave contemptibly, or did he offend him? No. The reasons were two essays Kundera wrote: 'A Kidnapped West, or Culture Bows Out' and 'An Introduction to a Variation'. In the latter Kundera discusses the year 1968, and how the Russians (he writes 'the Russians', not the USSR) occupied his 'small country', banned his books and left him without any means of survival. A director wanted to help Kundera and suggested he write a stage adaptation of Dostoyevsky's novel *The Idiot*. Around this time, the occupiers stopped Kundera in his car one day. Nothing terrible hap-pened, after a search they let him go, and the Russian officer said in parting, 'This is all just a misunderstanding. Everything will be fine. We love the Czechs. We love you.'

Once he read *The Idiot*, Kundera realized that he would rather die of starvation than adapt Dostoyevsky's 'world of exalted gestures, gloomy depths, and aggressive sentiment-ality'. Kundera felt a tie between that unbearable world and the Russian tank driver who crushed his homeland, only to go around telling Czechs how much Russians love them, forcing them to accept this love and live the way the occupiers wanted them to. And there you have it, that mysterious Russian soul.

In 'A Kidnapped West', Kundera directly echoes Czesław Miłosz by approaching this theme more broadly. He considers Central Europe in its entirety, including all those 'small' countries, geographically in the centre, that have belonged to the West culturally for centuries and ended up in the East politically, under Moscow's control, after the second World War. That is the tragedy of Central Europe, for whom Russia's anti-Westernism is self-evident. And that is why the people of Central European countries most wanted to be part of the West, while the West didn't even notice they had been kidnapped. It is revealing that in his essay Kundera does not make any real distinction between the descriptions 'Russian' and 'Soviet'. He realizes that for an anti-Communist Russian (for example, Solzhenitsyn) an abyss lies between his idealized Russia and the Bolshevik USSR, but why should this matter to the subjugated 'small' nations? Because really (I can attest), when someone wants to suffocate you in imperial embraces of great pathological love, what difference does it make whether it is being done by the Tsar-*batiushka*, the General Secretary of the Communist Party, or the bald *Khuilo*? Your – our – task is to break out of these embraces, at any cost.

This was something the imperialist Brodsky could not forgive. First Kundera, then us. After all, there is bitter irony in a Russified Jewish man mounting a defence of an antisemite by writing the troubled article 'Why Milan Kundera is Unfair to Dostoyevsky'. Brodsky declared with all the national pride of a Great Russian that the West has never given the world a writer as deep as Fyodor Mikhailovich, and strove to prove that a Russian soldier and Russian culture are not intertwined in any manner. And, of course, Brodsky's reaction to our independence is truly disgusting when he wrote in his poem that there is '. . . no reason to spoil blood, to tear the clothes off your chests', and that, 'when it comes time for you to die, you cattle, you'll mutter, tearing at your deathbed, the verse of Aleksandr and not the bullshit of Taras.'*

So, Joseph, thanks to your spiritual countrymen, once again it is 'time for us to die', once again you make us bleed and you tear the clothes off our women's chests. And here's what comes to many of our minds: first, let God, or fate, or whoever, send us anything but your love. Second, there is at least one fundamental trait common among Russian culture and a Russian soldier, which (somewhat paraphrasing Stanisław Lem) can be characterized by the word 'excrementalism'. Only a Russian soldier leaves piles of faeces in our buildings while destroying us, while Russian culture soils our heads and our souls. And, third, no, we won't mutter your Aleksandr Pushkin. When Kalibr and Iskander missiles shoot out of a clear sky onto residential districts, people seldom have time to pick which poem to read. But hopefully you were able to, and hopefully with your final breath you were able to recite 'To the Slanderers of Russia'† or some other drivel. You promised to die on Vasylievsky island, but you died in Brooklyn. You lied. As always, you lied.

Translated by Mark Andryczyk

---

* Ukraine achieved independence on 24 August, 1991. Joseph Brodsky wrote the poem 'Na nezavisimost ukrainy' ('On the Independence of Ukraine') in the early 1990s. This essay refers to fragments from that poem.
† A patriotic poem by Aleksandr Pushkin written in 1831.

The God-to-Human Phrasebook

Taras Prokhasko

28 July 2022

I suspect that birds which eat whole cherries, pits and all, sense they are helping to sow seeds. The divine sorrow of seeking a purpose must become more bearable when helping to create some other form of life aberrant to simple genetics beyond the simple reproductive instinct. Birds see how trees grow from their droppings, in places they only could have grown with the help of birds flying on a full stomach.

I don't want to startle anyone, but I am thoroughly convinced that people sense the same thing. Transporting plant seeds to any spot on Earth is a pretty good analogue to the ritual of the Divine Liturgy, available to anyone who is sad because they do not have sufficient initiation in the mystery to have the right to administer the sacrament.

Plants, from seeds to their natural or violent death, comprise a sign system that leads, pushes, carries, presses out and dislodges the helplessness inherent in the first sign systems a person possesses. To take it to the maximum degree, plants are special chapters in the God-to-human phrasebook. *What* people understand is one thing, *how* they understand is another. This phrasebook doesn't concern itself with materiality. Plants are simply a language that is heard and spoken.

Anyway – we don't know why – this year, this spring and

summer at least (autumn has not yet shown itself, autumn has not yet appeared, is not yet in our lives and may not happen, though the plants are screaming that all will be as it has always been), the interest of our people in diverse cultivation of plants has grown remarkably. Perhaps the sorrow has become acute. Plants, the first ingredient in any private liturgy, can lead you along a conspicuously marked path from the unbearable to the sweet.

Plants indicate how real you can be, how ready you are for the unexpected, how rooted you are, how migratory, how transitory, and at the same time how eternal you are. How little you need to live well. That it is impossible to exist without a few small, necessary things. Plants tell us what it's like to be a seed waiting to be carried to a random or chosen spot on Earth.

We hold microscopic and giant seeds in our hands. Even here, they anticipate everything. It's frightening to listen to the quiet sounds encased in their skins. We place them in the Earth. We talk to them about the mysteries of our sorrow. And soon – if you haven't abandoned your preacher yet – they sprout and you learn a few phrases from the God-to-human phrasebook. But you are no longer capable of answering.

In April of this year, one man, expecting conscription, hesitated to plant his garden. Who would this garden be for? A woman told him that he should sow them all. Let them grow. Anyone who arrives will find it. It has always been that way . . .

Let's say my grandmother, who, in captivity in Siberia, planted onions in small beds. She cultivated the space and received a signal that life multiplies the proof of life. The *Moskals** hated her. They crawled to her and pleaded with her

* *Moskal* is a Ukrainian pejorative for a Russian.

to give them just one scallion stem to snack on with their vodka. They were happy that someone had a scallion. Later they hated her again for having scallions. This is another chapter of the short and perplexing God-to-human phrasebook.

Or that beautiful woman from Babyn who managed to survive in forests and hideouts for months, living on a handful of dry bean seeds, left by chance in the pocket of her *serdak** jacket, which she managed to grab when fleeing from her house under the military's onslaught.

Translated by Michael M. Naydan and Alla Perminova

---

* A short, lightweight, long-sleeve jacket commonly worn by the Hutsuls in the Carpathian Mountains.

Herstory

Sophia Andrukhovych

28 July 2022

She sits across the aisle from me. She's fairly short and her hair is slicked back. She's wearing a stylish black shirt loose over wide black trousers. She talks on the phone a lot. She is businesslike and energetic, her low voice confident. She reports on how things are going. She is promising someone that she will come back soon and describes the contents of a fridge in detail. Then she instructs someone else, painstakingly and at length, how to care for a boxwood plant. Her tips are clear and precise. One bucket of water per metre of the shrub's height.

The border guard is gathering the passports and confirming that every photo matches the face of its holder. The bus is invariably filled with women, if you don't count the one teenage boy travelling alone to visit his mother, the five-year-old son of one of the passengers and the drivers. Up ahead are ten more buses. Only women can be seen from the windows. They scurry back and forth, knead their numb feet, gather in groups or smoke alone. A line of women queues patiently for the men's room.

The border guard flips through the woman in black's passport.

'When did you leave the temporarily occupied territories?' he asks.

A tense silence hangs in the carriage. No one budges, all

napes and backs are still, but the suffocating air in the bus thickens. Curiosity, tension, anxiety.

'In 2014,' the woman responds. She speaks loudly, so everyone can hear. Everyone. She wants to show that she is not afraid of anything, that she has nothing to hide. Her voice contains a challenge.

'And when do you plan on returning?' The young man in uniform continues the interrogation, respectfully, with just a hint of irony.

Once again – silence.

'After the victory, of course,' she says, trying to reply in Ukrainian, speaking with a Russian accent.

'After whose victory over whom?' The border guard mimics her pronunciation.

The silence intensifies.

'Wait. Wait a second. Wait. I'll show you.' The woman's voice becomes somewhat quieter, as if something has landed on her chest with a thud. She once again speaks in Russian.

She finds something on her phone and turns the screen towards the border guard.

'There you go,' she says.

The young man looks at it silently. His head has tilted so low that it looks like his chin is touching his chest.

'Do you know who they are?' she asks. The border guard does not reply. It's as if he knows the answer and doesn't want to voice it.

'These are my children,' the woman says.

Finally, the young man says, 'Forgive me. Please.'

The woman has put her phone away already and sits quietly, turning her face to the window, seemingly calm. As if she has already forgotten about that young man in uniform. She is so deep in her own thoughts that she no longer hears him.

He addresses her softly, almost in a whisper. It's as if he is trying to straighten things out, smooth over his own transgression.

'Try to understand,' he says. 'Recently, some lady coming from the same place as you tried to cross the border here. We took her aside for inspection. We found out that she was identifying places for rockets to bomb Lviv. You understand?'

The woman in black nods indifferently, not taking her gaze away from the window. The border guard completes his inspection of the passengers' passports in complete silence.

What was on that photograph? It wasn't for us to know. We could try to imagine the photo on the screen of the smartphone on which her children are suspended. Were the children smiling? Were they boys or girls? Were they little, or older? Which moment in their lives had this photograph captured? Was *this* a moment of life?

What we did know was that we would never know the story of the woman dressed in black and her children. Also known, without words, plucked from the air itself and felt most certainly among us all, was that the children in the photograph were not waving flags, not smiling, not packing humanitarian aid in crates, not posing joyfully with their friends. That knowledge hung in a heavy, dark silence.

Usually people never stop jabbering on these buses. They fill up with life stories, people sharing experiences of how and when the war entered their lives. A woman from Kharkiv admits that she vomited when she saw Russian tanks, right in the street; a woman from Dymer complains that she was just finishing renovating her house, it had taken years, she was putting up wallpaper when she was forced to flee her village; a young woman from Vinnytisa divulges that she is the only female member of her territorial defence group, and her boyfriend is very jealous.

Are these stories coming from women's mouths different from those voiced by men? Most likely, yes. One can assume that the men's stories would tell the impossibilities of retreating from one's own home and what lies behind those impossibilities, about rapidly diminishing options, about sacrificing one's own way of life in order to put that very life and one's own body at risk. They would testify to changes in their mind and transformations of their ego, about redrawing the borders of fear, about the meaning of the words 'bravery', 'dependability', 'dignity', and also 'hatred', 'cruelty' and 'revenge', about what it's like to be a hair away from death, and about death itself.

Perhaps the women's stories would be filled with longing for loved ones and would be saturated with fear for their children. They would talk about the silence of empty homes and the anguished, sleepless nights spent anticipating the sound of announcements, about rape and violence, about the difficulty and shame of talking about those things at all, and the frustration of rebuilding life within chaos and uncertainty. They would say a lot about love, even more about love and loss, including the loss of the life they once had.

The women's stories would also include bravery, hatred, sacrifice, and death, which is always nearby, and the men's would also contain love, great love, and fear and indecision, and sorrow for everything lost. No theme belongs exclusively to women or to men. The words themselves can be similar. The only difference is the voice.

*

'I know that he is your only one. But believe me, when you have more than one it doesn't get any easier.' If you could taste a voice, everyone who heard this voice would be stunned by its bitterness.

'When there are more of you and something terrible happens, you are all in it together, but it also multiplies,' she said.

'My oldest got depressed when he found out. He and Lionia always were very close, like twins. I knew that he was going to go to the enlistment office soon and that I wouldn't be able to handle it. The other one, my third, I went to his workplace, he's an ambulance nurse, and asked his bosses to give him the most difficult tasks, so he wouldn't have any free time to think.

'I went there, to that cursed Lukashivka, to that hell. Such a nice village. I went up to people and asked around. They'd already got to know the young men. They told me many things, about how they fed the young men and helped them. They loved our guys, you know. You can go there and ask around. I want to go there again when I get back from my daughter's place. I am drawn there. You want to go together? We'll go and ask about Dima again.

'Sasha is also studying to be a medic. Back in 2014, when it all began, he was studying for his entrance exams right there in the trenches. And he got in.

'You know, since I was sent their things, it's been over two months, I haven't washed their clothes. I lay Lionia's shirt and Sasha's shirt out on the bed and breathe in the scents, their dear scents, hug them, lie down, cry, and fall asleep.

'I don't want anything, I have no strength. I have two girl-friends in Kalush. They planted a garden for me and said: that's it, now you have to look after the garden. And just yesterday they brought me limewash and we painted the walls of another room in the building. A commission is supposed to visit us next week. We've submitted documents so that we can take in a few kids that have lost their loved ones. Maybe it's temporary, maybe their loved ones will be found, but let the children live with us in the meantime. If they're not found, we'll be their loved ones. I would really like that. I want to do this for my boys.

'You know, sometimes when I am grazing my cow I lie down in the grass and gaze. There a little insect is crawling along a stem: what elegant whiskers it has, what wonderful little paws. And I think to myself: no, it's not possible that God has taken care of the tiny whiskers of an insect but has abandoned my children. That can't be. He hasn't abandoned them. He's taking care of them.'

Translated by Mark Andryczyk

My Longest Text Message

Taras Prokhasko

10 August 2022

I don't get depressed but I do get excited by intellectual issues, both strategic and tactical ones, in my world view. But our daily life is filled with practical things from which we cannot retreat: a small child who is in need of more and more words and sentences, an ageing mother who needs both personal care and somehow – again – verbal care: you have to say something to her, to speak to her somehow. We don't have enough resources for this microcosmic world. There just isn't enough time and energy to take care of both your mother and your child. But we must take care of them when fully fledged war is being waged in our homeland. Anyone who faces difficulties knows that they will carry on even when things get yet more difficult. No matter how eager you are to fight on the front lines, you can't leave your part of the front, which plays as important a part in the war as any other.

Ukraine is experiencing an existential crisis. Russia is trying to destroy Ukraine. It doesn't want to take our resources or settle its people on our fertile lands; it wants to make Ukraine disappear. It doesn't just want to get rid of our intellectuals, it even wants to destroy our senior citizens, even though they might have mobility problems or dementia, along with our 'unenlightened' children who, for some reason, speak

Ukrainian to their parents. It wants Ukrainian books to vanish, along with documents, memories, ambitions, and the ability to say in Ukrainian – I am, I am this.

For more than a decade I have been annoyed by a particular trend in literature or, to be more precise, in cinema. They fabricate dangerous lies even when they adhere strictly to the facts. The past, regardless of whether it is the twelfth century or the nineteenth, or even the end of the twentieth, acquires the character of the year when a film is made. Morality and ethics are shown only through the paradigm of our modern times. The effect of this is devastating: it dilutes consciousness and kills the ability to feel what reality truly is.

Something similar is happening in the Russian – Ukrainian war. It is so archaic that we cannot explain it. Despite rich and complex histories, today's European peoples, nations, countries and states do not dare to assume that certain things that were last quite understandable in that part of Europe one thousand, three hundred, a hundred or eighty years ago can be happening right now, so nearby. It takes more than just empathy and compassion to ride this time machine. It requires conscious memories of skills and reflexes, of fears and horrors, of the divine value, of the divine pricelessness, of the divine futility of human life. You must imagine not the egocentric, but the historical perception of each person. To become yourself to lose yourself. To dissipate and emerge from nothingness.

The checkmate, stalemate, *gardez la reine*, of Ukrainian culture is that it is the main cause of the war. This culture, which has been evolving not in contempt of others but in the calm confidence of its own right to exist, has become the cause of a complex and gradual process of Ukrainian self-identification. It has ceased to be a ghetto culture. Its own contagiousness has doomed it to be the main target of aggression. Russia – all of Russia, not just a handful of Putinists – cannot tolerate the existence of a self-defined Ukraine. Russia, which has destroyed hundreds of intrinsically valuable cultures, which despises all other peoples that it has not yet destroyed (Germans, Poles, Americans, among others), which shows the greatest cruelty to its own people, which is most happy to be destroying itself (the best proof of which is all great Russian literature), has one major weakness. It loves Ukraine so much that it hates Ukrainianness above all. Denial of Ukrainianness is the basic essence of Russia.

Therefore, we, Ukrainians, are faced with two paths: to not be Ukrainians and suffer like the Russians, or to be Ukrainians, because this is who we are. And then there is war. Self-defence, like Krav Maga. This is peace. Ukrainian culture, for which we are dancing this deadly tango, cannot be pacifist. You can ask in the worst Balkan brothels – don't you girls love sex?

Nevertheless – and this is crucial – culture in war is not only about war. Life goes on. It is multifaceted, though it is divided into many pieces, like a pomegranate. There are those at the front and those who are far away. There are the itinerant and there are those who stayed at home. It is almost impossible to put a pomegranate back together. But you can pick out all the intact blood-red seeds and lay them on a plate. Mix them up, stir them with your eyes closed, trusting your fingers, so that no one can tell where each pomegranate seed used to be.

Translated by Alla Perminova and Michael M. Naydan

The Ouroboros Path

Iryna Tsilyk

23 August 2022

Let's be honest: more than anything, we want to feel pro-tected. All of us, or most of us, would prefer to rely on the old, civilized world, with its age-old system of relationships and values. We want to make plans for the future and build a clear pyramid of our needs – from the basic desire to breathe clean air, eat healthy food and make love, to the blurred and there-fore even more beautiful needs of self-expression, creativity, and so on. We want to build our own nests and give birth to children in places where our family trees have their roots and are fruitful, or vice versa – to freely travel the world, like Howl's Moving Castle. We want to work and study under the clear laws of a democratic society where we at least under-stand the general rules of the game. We want to have the right to freely choose our professions, religions, sexual partners, hair colour, skirt length and anything else. We want to know that we have something to fall back on, and we want to be sure that the books written by our predecessors so long ago contain all the necessary clues we might need. But war destroys the understandable world and leaves behind a burn-ing void, and there is no longer any point looking for simple answers.

Thousands killed and maimed, millions of perplexed

refugees with clenched teeth, mass graves, people medievally tortured, women raped barbarically, men and children, captives kept in inhumane conditions . . . the world broke once again and revealed its ancient, rotten, black guts. Let's be honest: you and I are no longer protected. We were never protected.

Here I am, lying in my warm comfortable bed, with a new orthopedic mattress; it's so comfortable. But there's one problem – the door to my room is unlocked, and for some reason this worries me. There is no lock, no keys – why do I need keys to a room in my own house when there are no strangers here? I am alone in this bed, but, it's odd, I remember I have a husband . . . but no, he's not around now. I hug both pillows with my sleepy hand. The night is quietly ticking away, barely audible, tall chestnut trees by the window are swaying in the wind and whimsical shadows crawl along the wall.

The door opens with a quiet creak and I think, something must be done with these hinges, why can't I fix the doors in my own home while my husband is away? But in the next moment I feel numb as I sense the thick heavy smell of a body that hasn't been washed for some time. The stranger approaches quietly and stands above me in silence. He has a large heavy body, a thick tangled beard, and a slow-witted muddy look. He looks like Turgenev's Gerasim, who drowned the poor dog Mumu; at least, that's how I imagined him. Very soon this alien body will probably rush at me, I think, press me to the bed with his immovable carcass, take out with a quick trembling hand what he has hidden in his pants and will fill my clean sheets with his heavy spirit . . . No! I start to scream blindly, but within a moment the sound of my scream mixes with an air-raid siren outside. It was just a dream, another terrible dream! I exhale with relief. There is no one in my house right now, not yet, and everything is fine.

Yes, everything is just f i n e. The siren sounds, like it does almost every night these days. My husband is somewhere at the front, he is a soldier again, and I am here in Kyiv. I move to the corridor leisurely – sleeping bags and pillows were stacked there last night in anticipation of an event like this. My twelve-year-old son emerges from his room, just as sleepily and calmly. No, it's not a bomb shelter, it's just a corridor. It breaks the naive rule of 'two walls' during shelling: this corridor won't protect us from a direct hit, but there are thick walls, no windows, and at least we won't be covered with glass during a possible blast wave. I turn my phone on and see that almost the whole of Ukraine is glowing red on screenshots of the missile-detecting app map on social media. This means that a missile can fly to any region, anywhere in my country, at any moment. This is what Russian roulette looks like now. But Kyiv hasn't been hit for a long time, at least a month or more, and since sirens sound over and over, almost every day, we don't go down to the basement every time we hear them. My fear of ending up trapped in the ruins of the basement, cut off from the exit, turns out to be much stronger than my fear of dying.

This brings to mind a story I heard recently, one that struck me. During regular shelling in Donetsk, a missile hit and destroyed a residential building. Dozens were killed and wounded, including children; the usual routine in our new reality. But for some reason, a story about one of the residents being caught in the bathroom by missile fire caught my attention. The man was taking a shower and didn't have time to hide. As a result of the damage to the building a concrete slab fell in such a way that the poor guy was trapped in a crevice. This man, completely naked, lay and waited for rescue for a long time. Thankfully he didn't wait in vain: rescuers freed him within twenty hours. He was luckier than that little six-year-old Ukrainian girl who, at the beginning of the full-scale war, also found herself under rubble and died there, not from her wounds but from dehydration. The rescuers didn't have time to reach her.

I'm lying on the floor of my corridor, my son is already snoring next to me, and I can't sleep for thinking about what that unfortunate girl and that man must have felt. Perhaps they prayed, as well as they could? Did they count the minutes? Did they try to remember both the brightest and most terrifying moments of their lives? Or perhaps they lay for countless hours in complete numbness, not allowing themselves to feel, think or hope. I can only guess at their thoughts and feelings, those poor people. But now I, and almost everyone around me, know a little about those moments when your whole life seems to be hanging off the edge of an abyss. Literally or figuratively. You lie there, trapped by circumstances, listening to your heartbeat, and the minutes slip away – drip, drip, drip . . . we are all very vulnerable, we are all, in fact, completely naked in the face of various dangers and our fears.

There has been a war in my country for many years. It destroyed our normal world for ever: it broke us, exhausted us, changed the way we look at familiar things. It taught us to be strong and fragile at the same time. We gradually got used to it, we continued to live, not just survive, and laughed, loved, travelled, created, searched for meaning, we went forward, blindly groping for the future. And we continue to, because war does not give any clues to when it will ever end. But the truth is that this war has already changed us. Subtly.

We are unprotected. We carry the trauma of insecurity as a stigma. It changes things a lot, actually.

My fears are always with me now. I am a tough twenty-first-century modern woman, mother of a teenager, wife of a very cool man, an artist, a feminist and more, but I carry these fears inside me, like an incurable disease that has already meta-stasized. Here, look, this is me, a 'tough modern woman' lying in the foetal position in the corridor who still can't get rid of the feeling of disgust from the memory of the stranger with an unwashed penis. Yes, it was just a nightmare, another agony from an endless series of my dreams. But what about others who've had to experience someone else's primitive desire to humiliate another human being, to destroy, to desecrate some-one else's body and spirit, to close someone's mouth, to tear tender flesh roughly, to 'punish' someone else, their dignity, their otherness, their right to say no? How many are there? I know some numbers. I saw the protocols and photos. I read testimonies. I heard personal confessions. I studied world his-tory, after all! Once upon a time, I read books and looked at the paintings of artists who were trying to comprehend the unthinkable desire of one human being to destroy another in the most terrible of ways, somehow.

Back then, in that other life, it all seemed so distant and unreal. But war and evil are always closer than they seem. When we meet it we are petrified, as if under the gaze of Medusa. Artists from the past, you knew it, you warned us.

In the winter, when anxious expectations of great calamity hung over my country once again, that is, when everyone around was talking about a possible full-scale invasion from Russia, the majority of Ukrainians continued to simply live. Yes, we were googling the news nervously, talking, as if telling jokes, about emergency escape-bags, planning possible scen-arios and what to do in the case of full-scale war. But at the same time we continued to work on our projects, went to the cinema and met friends, drank wine, entertained our children and stubbornly made plans, buying tickets for spring vacations. We knew and did not know, we believed and did not believe. How can you accept the idea that one day the army of another country can enter your home, breaking everything in its path, brutally raping and torturing innocent people and carrying mobile crematoria to burn the bodies of dissenters? How can you realize that images of a big terrible destructive war, familiar from childhood, can become reality for you and your family today? It is impossible. Yes, just recently there were wars in Syria, Georgia, Chechnya, the Yugoslav wars, Afghanistan and others, others. What can we say about the east of Ukraine, much closer, our land where the war that was not officially called a war has been going on for eight years? This all-too-real tragedy had already broken thousands of lives, and it changed my family's life too when my husband, a writer, joined the army.

I didn't really believe it. I was laughing somewhat nervously and drinking wine with friends. The wine was bitter. I remember at some point I started translating the poems of one of my favourite poets and stumbled upon one of his texts. It's a scary poem, actually. Complete suspense and anxiety. O what is that sound? the female protagonist asks. What is there, what is there? Why are those soldiers approaching us? Why? Many stanzas and refrains, unbearable anticipation which breaks through in the climax like an ancient abscess: *'O it's broken the lock and splintered the door, O its the gate where they're turning; Their boots are heavy on the floor, And their eyes are burning.'**

This poem was written in the 1930s. Like many others. We

---

* W. H. Auden, *Poems selected by John Fuller*, published by Faber & Faber. The poem 'O What is That Sound?' (1932), p. 12.

knew. We read. We saw the triumph of death, the disasters of war and in Guernica. We saw the burning eyes of enemies in our nightmares before. We all have collective anxiety sown into us at the genetic level. But now, in the twenty-first century, the heavy boots of the Russians are once again opening Ukrainian doors, and the whole civilized world is watching live.

How does one not become petrified? The war taught us to fear many things, so many different things that sometimes our life today feels like balancing on a tightrope between the very real faces of every phobia imaginable. What am I afraid of? I am afraid of being raped. I am afraid of pain, torture and mutilation. I am terribly afraid of being under occupation, in a trap where people like me or my husband or the rest of the people in our 'bubble' are put on special blacklists. Yes, it is true, people are hunted, people are imprisoned in basements, tortured by the same KGB methods as before, or by even more terrible, more primitive methods, the mere thought of which causes a modern person to feel chthonic horror. It was happening for at least eight years in the occupied territories of Ukraine, where terrorists set up torture and concentration camps for captured Ukrainians. And it is happening now, even more openly, already in the conditions of a full-scale war, in all senses of the word 'full-scale'.

There is also another category of fears. The fear of losing one's home, country, family is a blind horror deep-rooted in the tragedies of our grandparents and handed down to us as a legacy. Sent to the Gulag, victims of the Holocaust and Holodomor, tortured, powerless, broken people became the shadows of our ancestors, who follow us. Among them are my great-great-grandparents, who were exiled to the Solovki prison camp in the 1930s. By some miracle my great-great-grandmother managed to escape from the train station and went on to live a long and difficult life. But she never saw her husband again, and we don't know the details of his death in the Stalinist camps. There are many such stories, almost every Ukrainian family has them.

Sometimes you just want to flee from this reality. You want to run away from the world behind your eyes, escaping the destructive force that mercilessly grinds up the lives and destinies of millions of 'small', invisible people. To flee from repression, poverty, hunger or missiles. To run away, leaving behind burnt bridges and devastated houses, which had been tended with love for so many years. To run quickly, grabbing only necessities, unable to put thousands of other things into the emergency suitcase; they seem unimportant for survival, but it is from unnecessary things that annals of individual families and their memories are written. To run, grabbing our children, focusing on the animal fear and desire to protect them, frantically trying to fight for their survival and their future. Among all the shades and nuances of refugee trauma, the most painful for me is the burden of parents' responsibility for the lives of their children and, more globally, for the children of their nation.

Look, here is a person drowning in the fast water of the unknown and irreversible, but until the end this woman holds a child above her in her outstretched arms. Saving the most important, saving even at the cost of one's own life, not to suffocate from fear when we (yes, the adults are now us) have to act confidently, make decisions, row against the current, until the last breath.

I will never forget the moment I finally felt like this adult. On the second day of the full-scale Russian invasion a shell hit an ammunitions truck near my home. It detonated and then exploded for a long time, and the terrible deafening sound of imminent danger and the unknown was frightening. What is happening, what exactly is happening?! we were thinking, but there was no answer in that moment. I saw my child's primal, uncontrolled fear for the first time. He was shaking. That night I decided to take my son somewhere. My husband was going to join the army again, and the Sisyphus stone of responsibility fell on me. Here is your stone, woman, and here is your mountain.

We went to a safer place for a while but eventually returned home, we didn't wait for the war to end. Looking back, I realize that there are too many sharp corners within the irrational desire to flee or, conversely, to return. There are no simple answers to the question of how best to act. Go or stay? Press the pedal and rush forward, or stop and wait? To stay in my city and listen to air alarms, in real danger, or to flee to a well-fed and prosperous Europe and feel like lonely refugees, with all the associated traumas of homelessness? How to protect your children from all possible traces of this war?

Obviously, somewhere out there in distant worlds, in some cases you can save your life, but not save yourself. Or vice versa. It happens very differently. But one way or another, sometimes this choice simply doesn't exist, because there is nowhere to return. Let's say my best friends' house was destroyed by shelling. Later their town was freed from the occupation, they could return now, somehow rebuild their home, but they don't want to. During the occupation their murdered neighbours were simply buried in their gardens. How can you go back to a town that has been turned into a cemetery?

Well, we are lying in our corridor again. Drip, drip, drip – the time before the air alert is lifted is ticking away too slowly. I lie down and think, how should I go on? But let's be honest:

there won't be any hints. You and I both know that human history has been defeated, that the sages of the past can't teach us, the people of the present, anything, certainly not how to hope for a future. The entire history of world experience, centuries-old culture, all our skills and tools of modernity powerlessly surrender the moment a six-year-old girl dies under the ruins of her own house from dehydration. Or the moment a young man goes to the store to buy some food and a missile hits his house and kills his wife and their newborn baby. Or the moment soldiers force a mother to watch her child being raped. There are so many of these moments, and others, perhaps even more terrible, that a daily black routine is already formed from them. The most frightening thing about war is that you can get used to everything.

But it is necessary to go on somehow. And as much as people scare me, others inspire me. There is a power in people that moves mountains and destroys cruelty. A power in people no one in the old world saw coming. Those people who fight not only for their land, but also for their identity, the collective self, because our enemy wants to destroy exactly that, they want to enact a genocide of Ukrainians. Our neighbours want to see us weak and dead; this doesn't leave much room for compromise. And that's why almost everyone around me has learnt to face their fears and move forward. If necessary, they take up arms or volunteer, work and donate to the needs of our army, turn from designers and poets into military paramedics, they provide psychological assistance to war victims, and so much more. My grandmother, for example, used to go to the volunteer centre and weave camouflage nets for the front, until she passed away. There are many ways not to become petrified.

One of them is to tell stories, too. Books, paintings, films and so on could talk about us, deal with the pain and light the way in our search for life during and after the war. Art doesn't protect us from bullets, torture, rape and other tools of destruction. We've been walking in circles for many centuries and in this endless dance we bite our own tail like an ouroboros, a snake eating its tail. Maybe the point is that the ouroboros is trying in vain to look itself in the eye? That's how humanity spins, as if stung. And only culture, art, gives us this superpower, holding up a mirror to our tired eyes.

My phone suddenly vibrates – the air alarm is over, we can crawl back to our beds. The night ends, and with it the unbearable nightmares and waiting for dawn. Another night where I, holding the frightened child-deep-inside-of-me in my outstretched arms, swam out and didn't drown. It's time to make coffee and spin further, in a circle, in a circle, in a circle, like all people do.

Original English-language text edited by Mark Andryczyk

Author and Translator Biographies

Author Biographies

Sofia Andrukhovych (b. 1982) is a writer from Ivano-Frankivsk. She has written three books of short prose, three novels, one children's book and numerous essays. Her novel *Felix Austria* (2014) won the BBC Ukrainian Book of the Year award, and in 2015 she was awarded the Joseph Conrad-Korzeniowski prize. Her latest novel, *Amadoka* (2020), weaves together the histories of the ongoing war against Russia, the Stalinist repressions of the 1930s and the Holocaust in Ukraine.

Yuri Andrukhovych was born in 1960 in Ivano-Frankivsk, Ukraine. In 1985, he founded the literary performance group *Bu-Ba-Bu* (*Burlesk – Balahan – Bufonada* i. e. Burlesque – Bluster – Buffoonery). He has published five poetry books, seven novels and four books of essays. Yuri Andrukhovych's books are translated into twenty-two languages. He is a laureate of several prestigious international literary awards.

Oleksandr Boichenko is a literary critic, publicist, essayist and translator. From 1995 to 2008 he taught foreign literature and literary theory at Chernivtsi University. He has received the Gaude Polonia scholarship from Poland's Ministry of Culture three times. He is the author of nine books, including the award-winning *A Sort of Chautauqua* (2003) and *More or Less* (2015). He is a prolific translator from Polish into Ukrainian.

Andriy Bondar is a poet and translator. He was born in 1974 in Kamianets-Podilskyi. He studied history and literary theory at the National University of Kyiv-Mohyla Academy. He is the author of four collection of poetry and four collections of short stories. He is well known in Ukraine as a translator from Polish and English into Ukrainian and was an editor of the multilingual Facebook community Eurolution.Doc (Ukraine on Maidan) from January to April 2014.

Olena Huseinova (b. 1979) holds an MA in Philology from Kyiv-Mohyla Academy. She is the author of two books of poetry. Currently she works as a radio host and radio producer at the Public Broadcasting Company of Ukraine, UA:Radio Culture (UR-3) – the third channel of Ukrainian public radio. Since 26 February 2022, Olena has been working as a live host for the radio version of the 24-hour United News Marathon.

Taras Prokhasko studied biology at Lviv University and took part in student protests for Ukraine's independence in 1989–91. He is the author of eleven books. Prokhasko's books have been translated into English, Polish, Russian, Serbian and Czech. In 2020, for his collection of essays *Yes, However* he was awarded the prestigious National Taras Shevchenko Prize of Ukraine. He lives and works in Ivano-Frankivsk.

Volodymyr Rafeyenko is a Ukrainian writer, poet, translator and literary and film critic. Having graduated from the Donetsk University with a degree in Russian philology and culture studies, he wrote and published entirely in Russian. Following the outbreak of the Russian aggression in Ukraine's east, Rafeyenko left Donetsk and moved to a town near Kyiv, where he wrote *Mondegreen: Songs about Death and Love (2019)*, his first novel in the Ukrainian language.

Olena Stiazhkina is a Ukrainian writer. Until the Russian occupation in 2014, she lived in Donetsk, where she taught in the history department at Donetsk National University. After fleeing occupation, she abandoned the Russian language in favor of Ukrainian. She has written novels and collections of essays in addition to academic work. In 2021, she published the novel *Smert' Leva Sesila mala sense* (Cecil the Lion Had to Die).

Iryna Tsilyk (b. 1982) is a Ukrainian filmmaker and writer, based in Kyiv. She is the director of the award-winning documentary film *The Earth is Blue as an Orange* and the fiction film *Rock. Paper. Grenade*, based on the novel *Who Are You?* by Ukrainian writer, and Iryna's husband, Artem Chekh. Moreover, Iryna Tsilyk is the author of eight books (poetry, prose, children's books) published in Ukraine.

Translator Biographies

Mark Andryczyk has taught Ukrainian literature at Columbia University and administered the Harriman Institute's Ukrainian Studies Program since 2007. His is the author of *The Intellectual as Hero in 1990s Ukrainian Fiction* (2012). Andryczyk is editor and compiler of *The White Chalk of Days: the Contemporary Ukrainian Literature Series Anthology* (2017). His latest translation is Volodymyr Rafeyenko's novel *Mondegreen: Songs about Death and Love* (2022).

Michael Naydan is Woskob Family Professor of Ukrainian Studies and Professor of Slavic Languages and Literatures at The Pennsylvania State University in University Park. He works primarily in the fields of Ukrainian and Russian literature and literary translation. He has published over fifty articles on literary topics, more than eighty translations in journals and anthologies, and more than forty books of translations and edited volumes.

Alla Perminova is a practicing literary translator based in Barcelona, Spain. She received her doctoral and postdoctoral degrees in translation studies from Taras Shevchenko National University of Kyiv where she taught for fifteen years. She is the author of seventy scholarly articles, co/translator and/or editor of twenty books. Her personal philosophy as a translator and a researcher is discussed in her book *A Translator's Reception of Contemporary American Poetry.*

Acknowledgements

I would like to thank Michael M. Naydan and Alla Perminova for their translations for this volume. As always, I am very grateful to Yaryna Yakubyak for her suggestions on my translations.

Miriam Cahn, ma pensée sérielle by Irina Tsilyk published in French by Flammarion for the Palais de Tokyo exhibition in Paris, March 2023.

The original, Ukrainian-language versions of these essays were published as follows:

Andrukhovych, Sofiia. 'Simplicity' In *Dwutygodnik.com*, 14 July 2022.

Andrukhovych, Sofiia. 'Herstory' In *Dwutygodnik.com*, 28 July 2022.

Andrukhovych, Yurii. 'Use zbuvaietsia?' In *Zbruč*, 4 March 2022.

Andrukhovych, Yurii. 'Pro kuli v potylytsiakh' In *Zbruč* 8 April 2022.

Andrukhovych, Yurii. 'Chomu obov'iazkovo Ilyich?' In *Zbruč*, 1 July 2022.

Andrukhovych, Yurii. 'Lysty vid sultana i nazad' In *Zbruč*, 15 July 2022.

Boichenko, Oleksandr. 'Vid Vladyvostoka do Lisabona' In *Zbruč*, 12 April 2022.

Boichenko, Oleksandr. 'Po tsei bik dobra i zla' In *Zbruč* 20 June 2022.

Boichenko, Oleksandr. 'Isterychne impers'ke bydlo' In *Zbruč*, 18 July 2022.

Bondar, Andrii 'Vid tsynky do polietylenu' In *Zbruč*, 16 May 2022.

Bondar, Andrii. 'Povne rozchynennia' In *Zbruč*, 31 May 2022.

Bondar, Andrii. 'Viina Hitlera' In *Zbruč*, 13 June 2022.

Bondar, Andrii. 'Zruchnosti ta tsinnosti' In *Zbruč*, 28 June 2022.

Huseinova, Olena. 'Tikai' 17 March 2022. Unpublished.

Huseinova, Olena. 'Soromno' In *Reporters*, 30 March 2022.

Prokhas'ko, Taras. 'Viina pochynaietsia pryvatno' In *Zbruč*, 24 February 2022.

Prokhas'ko, Taras. 'Vorozhinnia na riadkakh' In *Zbruč*, 14 April 2022.

Prokhas'ko, Taras. 'Do tebe, liuba richechko' In *Zbruč*, 28 April 2022.

Prokhas'ko, Taras. 'Imperii pomyraiut' ranishe' In *Zbruč* 30 June 2022.

Prokhas'ko, Taras. 'Nasinnieve bohosliv'ia' In *Zbruč*, 28 July 2022.

Prokhas'ko, Taras. 'Moia naidovsha sms' In *Zbruč* 10 August 2022.

Acknowledgements

Rafieienko, Volodymyr. 'Try vesny, dva zhyttia, odna viina' In *Posestry*, 28 April 2022.

Rafieienko, Volodymyr. 'Planuvannia mynuloho' In *Posestry*, 12 May 2022.

Rafieienko, Volodymyr. 'Blyzhni sady' In *Posestry*, 2 June 2022.

Stiazhkina, Olena. 'Shchodennyk viiny. P'iatyi tyzhden' dovhoho liutoho' In *Deutsche Welle* (*dw.com/uk*), 7 April 2022.

Stiazhkina, Olena. 'Shchodennyk viiny. Chetvertyi misiats' liutoho' In *Deutsche Welle* (*dw.com/uk*), 7 July 2022.

Tsilyk, Iryna. 'Kholodna Vesna' 15 April 2022. Unpublished.

ALLEN LANE
an imprint of
PENGUIN BOOKS

Also Published

Theresa MacPhail, *Allergic: How Our Immune System Reacts to a Changing World*

John Romer, *A History of Ancient Egypt, Volume 3: From the Shepherd Kings to the End of the Theban Monarchy*

John Rapley and Peter Heather, *Why Empires Fall: Rome, America and the Future of the West*

Scott Shapiro, *Fancy Bear Goes Phishing: The Dark History of the Information Age, in Five Extraordinary Hacks*

Elizabeth-Jane Burnett, *Twelve Words for Moss*

Serhii Plokhy, *The Russo-Ukranian War*

Martin Daunton, *The Economic Government of the World: 1933-2023*

Martyn Rady, *The Middle Kingdoms: A New History of Central Europe*

Michio Kaku, *Quantum Supremacy: How Quantum Computers will Unlock the Mysteries of Science – And Address Humanity's Biggest Challenges*

Dacher Keltner, *Awe: The Transformative Power of Everyday Wonder*

William D. Cohan, *Power Failure: The Rise and Fall of General Electric*

John Barton, *The Word: On the Translation of the Bible*

Ryan Gingeras, *The Last Days of the Ottoman Empire*

Greta Thunberg, *The Climate Book*

Peter Heather, *Christendom: The Triumph of a Religion*

Christopher de Hamel, *The Posthumous Papers of the Manuscripts Club*

Ha-Joon Chang, *Edible Economics: A Hungry Economist Explains the World*

Anand Giridharadas, *The Persuaders: Winning Hearts and Minds in a Divided Age*

Nicola Rollock, *The Racial Code: Tales of Resistance and Survival*

Peter H. Wilson, *Iron and Blood: A Military History of German-speaking Peoples since 1500*

Ian Kershaw, *Personality and Power: Builders and Destroyers of Modern Europe*

Alison Bashford, *An Intimate History of Evolution: The Story of the Huxley Family*

Lawrence Freedman, *Command: The Politics of Military Operations from Korea to Ukraine*

Richard Niven, *Second City: Birmingham and the Forging of Modern Britain*

Hakim Adi, *African and Caribbean People in Britain: A History*

Jordan Peterson, *24 Rules For Life: The Box Set*

Gaia Vince, *Nomad Century: How to Survive the Climate Upheaval*

Keith Fisher, *A Pipeline Runs Through It: The Story of Oil from Ancient Times to the First World War*

Christoph Keller, *Every Cripple a Superhero*

Roberto Calasso, *The Tablet of Destinies*

Jennifer Jacquet, *The Playbook: How to Deny Science, Sell Lies, and Make a Killing in the Corporate World*

Frank Close, *Elusive: How Peter Higgs Solved the Mystery of Mass*

Edward Chancellor, *The Price of Time: The Real Story of Interest*

Antonio Padilla, *Fantastic Numbers and Where to Find Them: A Cosmic Quest from Zero to Infinity*

Henry Kissinger, *Leadership: Six Studies in World Strategy*

Chris Patten, *The Hong Kong Diaries*

Lindsey Fitzharris, *The Facemaker: One Surgeon's Battle to Mend the Disfigured Soldiers of World War 1*

George Monbiot, *Regenesis: Feeding the World without Devouring the Planet*

Caroline Knowles, *Serious Money: Walking Plutocratic London*

Serhii Plokhy, *Atoms and Ashes: From Bikini Atoll to Fukushima*

Dominic Lieven, *In the Shadow of the Gods: The Emperor in World History*

Scott Hershovitz, *Nasty, Brutish, and Short: Adventures in Philosophy with Kids*

Bill Gates, *How to Prevent the Next Pandemic*

Emma Smith, *Portable Magic: A History of Books and their Readers*

Kris Manjapra, *Black Ghost of Empire: The Long Death of Slavery and the Failure of Emancipation*

Andrew Scull, *Desperate Remedies: Psychiatry and the Mysteries of Mental Illness*

James Bridle, *Ways of Being: Beyond Human Intelligence*

Eugene Linden, *Fire and Flood: A People's History of Climate Change, from 1979 to the Present*

Cathy O'Neil, *The Shame Machine: Who Profits in the New Age of Humiliation*

Peter Hennessy, *A Duty of Care: Britain Before and After Covid*

Gerd Gigerenzer, *How to Stay Smart in a Smart World: Why Human Intelligence Still Beats Algorithms*

Halik Kochanski, *Resistance: The Undergroud War in Europe, 1939-1945*

Joseph Sassoon, *The Global Merchants: The Enterprise and Extravagance of the Sassoon Dynasty*

Clare Chambers, *Intact: A Defence of the Unmodified Body*

Nina Power, *What Do Men Want?: Masculinity and Its Discontents*

Ivan Jablonka, *A History of Masculinity: From Patriarchy to Gender Justice*

Thomas Halliday, *Otherlands: A World in the Making*

Sofi Thanhauser, *Worn: A People's History of Clothing*

Sebastian Mallaby, *The Power Law: Venture Capital and the Art of Disruption*

David J. Chalmers, *Reality+: Virtual Worlds and the Problems of Philosophy*

Jing Tsu, *Kingdom of Characters: A Tale of Language, Obsession and Genius in Modern China*

Lewis R. Gordon, *Fear of Black Consciousness*

Leonard Mlodinow, *Emotional: The New Thinking About Feelings*

Kevin Birmingham, *The Sinner and the Saint: Dostoevsky, a Crime and Its Punishment*

Roberto Calasso, *The Book of All Books*

Marit Kapla, *Osebol: Voices from a Swedish Village*

Malcolm Gaskill, *The Ruin of All Witches: Life and Death in the New World*

Mark Mazower, *The Greek Revolution: 1821 and the Making of Modern Europe*

Paul McCartney, *The Lyrics: 1956 to the Present*

Brendan Simms and Charlie Laderman, *Hitler's American Gamble: Pearl Harbor and the German March to Global War*

Lea Ypi, *Free: Coming of Age at the End of History*

David Graeber and David Wengrow, *The Dawn of Everything: A New History of Humanity*

Ananyo Bhattacharya, *The Man from the Future: The Visionary Life of John von Neumann*

Andrew Roberts, *George III: The Life and Reign of Britain's Most Misunderstood Monarch*

James Fox, *The World According to Colour: A Cultural History*

Clare Jackson, *Devil-Land: England Under Siege, 1588-1688*

Steven Pinker, *Rationality: Why It Is, Why It Seems Scarce, Why It Matters*